KOSTYA

KOSTYA

From Russia With Gloves

Kostya Tszyu with Malcolm Andrews

ABC
Books

'By any measure, Kostya Tszyu's life and accomplishments are quite remarkable'

John Howard, Prime Minister of Austral

KOSTYA TSZYU

By any measure, Kostya Tszyu's life and accomplishments are quite remarkable. A second book devoted to detailing them is both warranted and welcomed.

Born and raised in tough surroundings, Kostya was attracted to Australia by the opportunities it offered. Aspects of his life and experience therefore have much in common with many other overseas-born Australians who have contributed so magnificently to the nation's cultural richness and development.

Where Kostya, of course, differs is in relation to his boxing skill and legendary achievements. Combining talent and discipline, Kostya has made the most of the opportunities afforded to him to become the first Australian boxer to unify a division, the first man in 40 years to unify the Super Lightweight division, and one of only three undisputed champions world-wide.

In the pursuit of his goals, Kostya has had to overcome a number of obstacles. In rising to meet these challenges, Kostya has displayed admirable determination, endearing himself to many in his adopted homeland. His achievements, and their recognition in the country of his birth, have brought an added dimension to Australia's relationship with Russia.

Through acknowledging the key moments in Kostya's life and career, this book pays tribute not only to Kostya, but also to those who have played their part in his remarkable success.

(John Howard)

CONTENTS

'Central to this young man's success has been the simple concept of family.'

Alan Jones

ALAN JONES

Top-rating Sydney breakfast radio personality for the past two decades. He began in radio after success as a teacher, speechwriter for Prime Minister Malcolm Fraser, and a Rugby coach, whose greatest contribution was steering the Australian Wallabies to victory against all four Home Nations on their 1984 tour of Great Britain and Ireland.

SUPREME TRIUMPH OF SPIRIT

I HAVE known Kostya since the day he arrived in Australia. It's impossible to think of a better story relating to the triumph of the human spirit and personal potential.

There have been many architects of that triumph. Of course, Johnny Lewis, the boxing coach without equal, has guided, fathered, supported and cajoled Kostya to international stardom.

But, in many ways, it's a simpler story than that. I remember Kostya telling me about the circumstances of his family back in Russia: the tiny room where they all lived together; the belief that boxing may emancipate his family; and the unshakable faith he had in his own ability to virtually free his family from the limitations of that life.

It's no surprise, therefore, that in spite of all the barriers he has met here, and there were many beyond that of language, Kostya is never beaten. He may be down, as he has been, with unfair reporting or legal collisions, but he's never beaten.

In boxing terms, Johnny has told me often that Kostya may be the best pound-for-pound boxer ever.

But I digress. Central to this young man's success has been the simple concept of family. And a night in Kostya's home is proof of that — Mum, Dad, Natasha, the kids, the toys, the pets (don't start me about the pets!). All of these are manifestations of a young man at ease with himself, proud of what he has achieved, determined not to let go of that success and dedicated to making sure that those he loves who have been with him on this wild ride will still have a reason to be with him when it ends.

In many ways, his victory over Sharmba Mitchell is the most emphatic statement of his unchallengeable championship status. Think of it in horseracing, tennis or swimming terms. Name a single champion — apart from the great racehorse Tulloch (who, in the 1950s returned, but a shadow of his former greatness) — who has vacated the seat at the highest level of sport and returned as emphatically victorious as Kostya was against Sharmba. They don't exist.

And that is why, whenever the history of Australian sport is written, and whenever the history of world boxing is written, the name of Kostya Tszyu will occupy an indelible place in bold type. Those of us who have known him well will remember, long after the victories fade, the supreme triumph of spirit, application and skill that has made Kostya an object lesson to many and a role model for those who seek success but often want to take short cuts with the effort.

Books of this kind are important to catalogue such a story.

9

PRELUDE

I AM A PROFESSIONAL BOXER. As such, two or three times a year I step into a ring with another man and try to physically tame him. Some people see boxing as a brutal pastime. I see it as a sport. I never have any animosity towards my opponent and usually when our fight is over we become the best of friends. We are warriors who give our all in the ring and respect each other out of it.

It was not that way in the first fight I can remember. I was about seven years old, back in my home town of Serov in Russia. It was a street fight with another kid. I can't remember what started it, a bit of argy-bargy, the two of us pushing and shoving each other. Suddenly, I lined him up and hit him with a series of the sweetest left-right combinations you could ever imagine. Boom, boom, boom! The other kid went down like a sack of potatoes and was out cold before he hit the ground. I was terrified about what I had just done … I hadn't meant to hurt him … it was just a street scuffle … it gave me a huge fright.

That night my Papa decided that if I was going to fight, I should learn boxing and channel my efforts in the ring, not on the street. At the age of seven, I went along to a gym for the first time. I didn't like it at all. So after one training session the boxing career of Kostya Tszyu was put on hold. Of course, I was too young. Most Russian boys never started in boxing until they were about 12 years old. But at the age of nine I was back in the gym and this time I was enjoying it. So began my life in boxing spanning the next quarter of a century. It was a career that would take me to world champion status both in the amateur ranks and as a professional. It would see my family and me move from a cramped one-room apartment in a grim Russian industrial town to a large, comfortable house in Australia's biggest city, Sydney.

There were to be many setbacks along the way. But I have always believed that to get what you want in life, you must overcome adversity. As a former Australian Prime Minister once said — life wasn't meant to be easy.

11

I was just four months old when this photo with Mama and Papa was taken

PROUD HERITAGE

JUST AS I AM PROUD to be Russian by birth and Australian by choice, I also have another heritage that fills me with pride — Korean. The name Tszyu comes from ancestors I know nothing about. And that's a real regret. My great-grandfather migrated from Korea to Russia around the start of the 20th century. No one in my family knows why. My grandfather may have known, but he apparently never talked about it and he died when my father, Boris, was just a teenager. Not that I blame him for keeping quiet. Most people who lived through the horrors of the Stalin era in the Soviet Union never volunteered details of their family's past. What is the World War II British expression? Loose lips sink ships. In Stalin's time those loose lips would have been a ticket to a gulag (concentration camp) or worse still a firing squad.

All I know is that my great-grandfather's family was broken up by the Stalinist authorities and forcibly scattered around the Soviet Union in 1937. My grandfather, Timophey Tszyu, ended up in Serov. I have since discovered another branch of the family in Tashkent. But as for the rest, I haven't a clue. Once you were in a certain town or city — that was usually where you stayed for the rest of your life. Under the communist system you did what the government told you to — be it in what job to work, where to live, or where to go on your holidays.

Soon after the death of his father, Papa started work as a locksmith in a Serov factory. He was just 16. When he was old enough he served his compulsory two years in the army before returning to the local steelworks where he worked from 7am to 4pm every day. Mama was a nurse and she used to work some ungodly hours in random

12 hour shifts. I started at kindergarten when I was 18 months old, so she could get back into the work force, and many a time I would have to sleep overnight at the kindergarten, because Papa would have left for work before Mama came home.

People in Australia cannot imagine in their wildest dreams what life was like for the Tszyu family at Flat 64, Number 8 Korolenko House (a two-storey building, divided into four apartments on a housing estate in Lobva, a suburb of Serov). Two families lived in each apartment. We got the worst deal in our apartment. The other family had been allocated two bedrooms, we had just one — and a tiny one at that. Into it Mama and Papa crammed all our worldly possessions. There was a single bed for my younger sister Olga, a second bed fractionally larger for Mama and Papa. As for me, I slept on the floor under a table. There was also a refrigerator and a wardrobe shoved into a couple of the

My Papa fishing with a mate during winter in the Urals

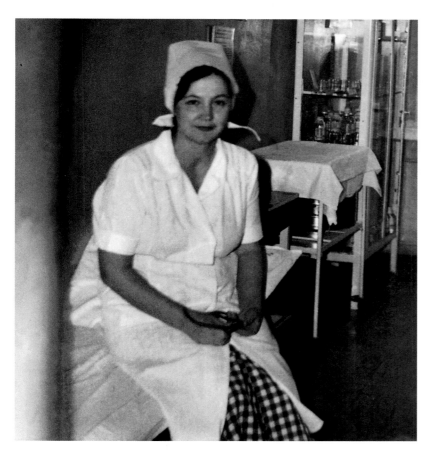

Mama working as a nurse in Serov in 1980

corners of the room. How everything fitted was a miracle. We shared the kitchen with the other family and there were often arguments about using the oven. There were also plenty of dramas every morning when we fought over the use of the one bathroom. Anyway, the local council used to turn off the water overnight and often it hadn't been switched on again when we were all rushing to get ready for work or school. We would go to a local community bathhouse two or three times a week to get properly cleaned. At busy times we would have to queue for up to an hour for our turn in the baths that held 100 people at a time. Every now and then, if we had a bit of spare money we could pay for the luxury of an individual bath. But that was a rare treat.

At nights, curled up under the table I would dream about becoming famous and taking my family away from this tiny room. An apartment all to ourselves ... just the four of us. Or maybe, if I was very, very, very famous, a house. How grand would that be! I never lost sight of that dream. I reckoned my parents deserved more than the cards they had been dealt by the Soviet system.

My father has always been my hero. People in Russia tell me Papa was good enough to have been an Olympic wrestler, but he never got the opportunity because he started work at such a young age. He had always been fast and strong — and even is today in his late 50s.

So instead of competing at the Olympics at Tokyo in 1964 or at Mexico City four years later, he was working to provide a future for his family that he expected would eventually be so dependent on him. I know he would have had the determination to succeed at the highestlevel in his chosen sport. That was one of the things he instilled in me. Determination. To this day I set myself goals and never give up until I achieve them. Too many people choose the easy way out.

15

Papa had been on a waiting list for an apartment of his own for 20 years. Because of queue jumping by people who had party officials as friends it took a long time for him to move from about number 400 on the list of those waiting to a position where we could move. When I was 13 … joy of joys … we were allocated a three-bedroom apartment. For Papa it was like winning Lotto would be to someone in Australia. It was no mansion, but we were over the moon. No more would we have to fight the neighbours every day for the bathroom. And Olga and I would each have our own bedroom and space in which to move!

Kids having fun. With a neighbour when I was about 4 years old

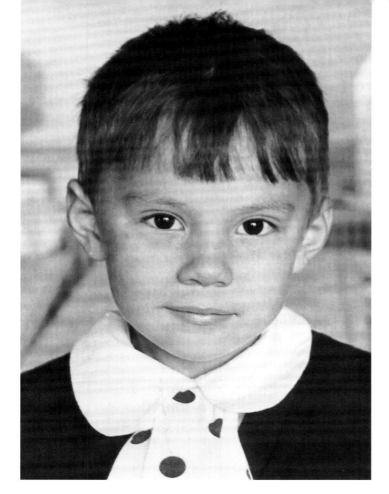

The first steps to greatness — the first three medals I ever won

At six years of age, butter wouldn't melt in my mouth

Olga and I in Serov

Taking the cold Siberian winds on the chin. Outside my old school in Serov, 1983

THE DIE IS CAST

I HAD MY FIRST OFFICIAL FIGHT when I was about 10. It was against a boy who was a couple of years older than me from another gym in Serov. It was over very quickly. I walked straight up to him and punished him with a few hard right-hand punches. Bam, bam, bam! But I might have got a bit too cocky with the ease of the win. I lost my second fight. Papa told me I must prepare my mind for each fight. It was no good being fast in the ring unless you were fast in the brain too.

French without tears. I wasn't really an enthusiastic student at school. I knew I was destined to be a factory worker if my boxing career ever faltered

I only had a few bouts with that first trainer because he soon left the gym. The fellow who trained some of my first opponents, Vladimir Chernya, heard about this and asked me to join his gym on the other side of Serov. The seeds were sown for a long and fruitful partnership. We remained together for the rest of my amateur career. Training with Chernya meant a lot of travel across the city. But what is the adage? Nothing of value comes without effort.

As a teenager I was pretty good at aerobics too

Trim, taut and terrific. All ready to rumble.

21

Snow business. If you live
in Russia, much of the
year your roadwork is
done in the ice and snow

A pair of aces — me and
coach Vladimir Chernya

Chernya was only in his mid-twenties so he became like a big brother to me. He taught me the importance of good boxing technique and how to know when to attack with crisp punches and when and how to defend against an aggressive opponent. That early grounding was the foundation for my later successes. Chernya also taught me in those early days the value of hard work and clever psychology. Both have served me well over the years. Hard work? I had to learn how to conquer pain. He would have me and the other kids in his gym running barefoot in the snow for periods of up to 15 minutes. In the end we had no feeling in our frozen feet.

'Concentrate, Kostya,' he would call out. 'Concentrate on the running and you will forget the pain. Concentration is the key to blocking out all pain. One day, you will thank me for this.'

In the gym he would push me to what I thought was my limit — and then past it. Regularly I would vomit into a bucket. But he would force me to train harder until I threw up a second time.

Two decades later as I started my preparation for each world title defence at the Australian Institute of Sport in Canberra I would still challenge my limits. And I would invite other young boxers to join me as they challenge theirs. Often they didn't know what hit them — they have never known such a gruelling training regimen.

And what about psychology? As Chernya explained: 'Be smart, Kostya. You're not as strong as these older fighters, so use your brain. Remember, Kostya, brain always beats brawn.'

I was about 14 when Chernya told me I had to make a big decision. Was I going to concentrate on my school studies or put all my efforts into boxing. I couldn't do both. There was really little choice. I had been a bit of a rebel at school — and I knew I had the potential to go all the way in the boxing ring. I decided there and then that one day I would represent my country in world championships and at the Olympics. I didn't want to follow the track that my Papa had journeyed — giving up a promising sporting career for a mundane life working in a factory. By becoming a champion boxer, I could perhaps make life easier for him and Mama. I wanted them never to have to worry about money again.

At 15 I won a Russian title, beating a 32-year-old boxer in the final. I was beaten in my first bout in the Soviet Championships — but I had shown enough to be invited to join the national team at a training camp. That same year I won my first international bout, against a Polish fighter. Things were going according to plan. I was a so-called amateur, but was earning more than Papa did at the factory.

At 16, there was more success. It came during the Soviet Junior Championships at K'ut'aisi, an historic city in Georgia. The first milestone was in the quarter-finals. I beat a fellow from Uzbekistan and, in doing so, achieved the status of Master of Sport in the Soviet Union — a rare honour for someone who was only 16. I carried on through the semi-final and despite being hit by a strange virus that sapped my strength on the eve of the final I managed to win the title. Looking back, the victory was probably the easy part. I was then faced with a 3000km journey home — a four-hour bus trip, followed by a three-hour plane flight and a 10-hour overnight train journey. But I couldn't have cared less about the discomfort, especially when I arrived home just before dawn and showed Papa the gold medal. I thought he was going to burst into tears. He had a certain spring to his step as he headed off to work that morning. But he was back an hour or so later. His boss had sent him home to celebrate my success. Chernya, who hadn't been at the championships with me, turned up to find out how I had fared. And he was over the moon too. He and Papa broke open a bottle of vodka that was soon demolished. They both finished with sore heads.

How did I do, coach?

OLYMPIC DREAMS SHATTERED

SOLDIER TSZYU. At the age of 18 every Soviet youth had to serve in the military. Being an elite sportsman I was fast-tracked through the system. Before I had even reached 18, I was put into Dynamo, the world-famous sporting organisation which was then attached to the KGB. In a Catch-22 situation you couldn't take the oath of allegiance until you were 18. But you couldn't be in military college without swearing the oath. In the end I spent only 20 days in uniform before heading back to boxing camp in late 1987.

At a theme park in Alushta with two other Soviet boxing hopefuls

The camp was at the Black Sea resort town of Alushta, the so-called 'Gateway to the Ukranian Riviera' on the Crimean Peninsula. It is so beautiful that it has inspired generations of great Russian painters. Sadly, I have bad memories of it. I contracted some virus that attacked my liver, which put me in hospital for two weeks. When I came out the boxing authorities refused to accede to my pleas to be excused from training until I had fully recovered, dropped me from the national squad and cut off my wages. It was a tough road back into favour. But I made it in time to challenge for a place on the team for the 1988 Seoul Olympics.

On my 18th birthday the Soviet boxing team made a special presentation to me. A year later the boxer who presented it, Yyacheslav Yanovsky, was to be a teammate of mine at the 1988 Seoul Olympics, and winner of the light-welterweight gold medal. His opponent in the final was Aussie Grahame 'Spike' Cheney. At 31 Yanovsky was too experienced for Spike, winning a unanimous points decision.

Back in uniform. Well, not quite. Just before the 1988 Seoul Olympics, I and a couple of other members of the boxing team met up with some guys from the navy in the city of Khabarovsk, near the border with Manchuria, and borrowed their caps for a photo.

I had been runner-up in the World Junior Championships in Havana in 1987, beaten by the reigning champion Juan Hernandez, who was urged on by tens of thousands of xenophobic fellow Cubans. I lost a close contest on points, even though I thought I had the better of the fight. There is a standard joke in amateur boxing uttered by fighters from all countries — to get a decision over a Cuban in Cuba you have to knock him out. But it was great preparation for the 1988 Seoul Olympics, as Hernandez is still regarded as one of the finest amateur boxers the world has ever seen, with gold medals in four world championships in the senior ranks — 1991 (in Sydney), 1993 (Tampere, Finland), 1995 (Berlin, Germany) and 1999 (Houston, USA).

Training often isn't a pretty sight. With the Soviet junior team at Mogilev in Belarus during 1986

In the lead-up to the Olympics, I was beaten in the final of the Soviet Championships by Orzubek Nazarov, who was later to turn professional and become World Boxing Association world lightweight champion. But then, just 17 days before the start of the Games, I suffered a major setback. And it didn't come in the boxing ring. The Soviet pre-Olympic training camp also involved cultural activities. I was acting in a play when a glass window next to the stage shattered and a sliver of glass sliced through the little finger on my left hand, severing the tendons. Normally it would take at least a month to heal, but with the Olympics so close that wasn't possible. The doctors considered amputating the finger, which would then heal in time, but decided against such a drastic measure. Instead I kept the injury secret from my opponents and fought my bouts in Seoul virtually using only my right fist. I won my first two bouts but was beaten in a split decision in the quarter-finals by the eventual gold medal winner, Andreas Zuelow of East Germany.

There were some strange decisions at Seoul — so strange that the whole method of judging amateur fights was later completely overhauled. The strangest of all involved Korean light-middleweight Park Si-hun who won the gold medal. The result of the final against American Roy Jones Junior, regarded by many experts as the greatest fighter pound-for-pound in the history of boxing — amateur and professional — has been ridiculed ever since. Jones landed 86 punches to Park's 32 in the three rounds. But the judges gave the bout to Park. The embarrassed Korean even apologised to Jones. One of the judges, Morocco's Hiourd Larbi, explained: 'The American won easily … so easily that I was positive my four fellow judges would give the fight to the American, so I voted for the Korean to make the score 4-1 and not embarrass the host country.' It transpired that the judges from Uganda and Uruguay felt the same way, and Park got the nod 3-2. I later became good friends with Roy Jones during his professional career and we trained together when years later he visited Sydney.

I talk about old times with the great Roy Jones Junior

THE LOVE OF MY LIFE

I WAS TO MEET THE LOVE OF MY LIFE in 1989. Natasha Anikina, three years younger than me, was a hairdresser who worked in a salon in Serov. We were among a group of teenagers who used to get together regularly to enjoy ourselves. It wasn't love at first sight. But it was to be a lasting love. When I used to go off to training camps or tournaments I quickly realised how much she meant to me and how much I missed her. I couldn't get back to Serov quickly enough. As I wrote at the time — one day she will be my wife and the mother of my children.

'Natasha is the rock on which my life is built'

Kostya

Love can be such a serious thing. You wouldn't believe it from the photograph … but we were very happy when photographed on our first date

Natasha's family in 1973 — her mother Valentina, a nurse, father Leonid, a truck driver, and brother Vova. Ironically, Valentina had gone through nurses' school with Mama and they worked in the same hospital in Serov

Natasha and her brother are well rugged up. After all, even in autumn it's cold in Russia. Their grandmother used to look after them a lot — and here they are outside her place

And how we change over the years. Two glamorous ladies — my sister Olga and my lovely wife dressed up for New Year's Eve celebrations to welcome in the new millennium

Five-year-old Natasha playing in the sandbox at kindergarten

After the Seoul Olympics I decided on a new hairstyle. I wanted something that would set me apart. A mate and I went to a salon in Serov and he and the hairdresser came up with the idea of one tuft of hair at the back that was longer than the rest. As they say ... the rest is history. When it grew longer and I wanted to keep it out of my face during fights I used to get members of my family to plait it. Now I can do it myself. It's been described as everything from a rat's tail to a pigtail to a ponytail. But, quite frankly, it's just 'my hair'.

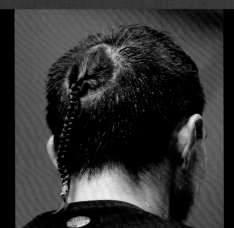

HAIR!

I won my second Soviet Championship gold medal in 1990, the year I went to the United States for the 1990 Goodwill Games in Seattle and took out the gold in the light-welterweight division. But I was still on a learning curve. I wrote in my diary before my first bout: 'As far as achieving my full potential, I am still a relative novice in the boxing game. It is like when a sculptor goes to work. He starts with a rough piece of marble knowing that eventually by chipping away at all the rough edges he will finish with a beautiful sculpture. So it is with me. I am still little more than that roughly hewn piece of marble. The finishing touches are still a long way from being applied.'

How ironic then that when I was back in America the following year for the traditional USSR v USA meeting I should visit Mount Rushmore National Memorial where the sculptor Gutzon Borglum had carved the giant faces of four US presidents — George Washington, Thomas Jefferson, Theodore Roosevelt and Abraham Lincoln — out of a mountainside in the Black Hills of South Dakota. Here are the two national teams with the four famous Americans looking down on us.

I could relate to Roosevelt. One of his most famous utterances was 'Speak softly and carry a big stick'. Throughout my career I was never a loudmouth. And the big stick? My two boxing gloves, of course.

A NEW LIFE

THE YEAR 1991 WAS ONE of the most successful of my amateur career. I began by winning the Soviet Championships at the Black Sea city of Novorosiysk. Next came a gold medal performance and boxer of the tournament in the European Championships in the Swedish city of Gothenburg. And finally came the ultimate — victory in the World Championships in Sydney. It was there that I realised I had nothing left to prove in the amateur ranks. I had climbed the mountain. I was on top of the world looking down. An Olympic gold medal would have been nice, but it would only be equal to the medal I had just won.

Joking around with Mama before heading off to training camp before the 1990 Goodwill Games in Seattle. You will notice the early variation of my now distinctive hairstyle. It's more like a parrot's beak than the 2005 variety

Ready to fight for
Mother Russia

A bouquet for my third Soviet Championship success in 1991

Waiting in the wings was Sydney promoter Bill Mordey and his good friend, trainer Johnny Lewis. Mordey offered me $100,000 to turn professional. It was a lot of money for a young kid from Serov. But it was not the money that eventually swayed me. It was the opportunity for a new life in Australia. My short stay in the beautiful harbour city had excited me. Mordey gave me $1000 for expenses and said he would send plane tickets for Natasha and me. Back in Serov I knew there could be only one answer to his offer. Yes! And straight after the Russian Orthodox Christmas (January 7), Natasha and I flew out of Moscow to begin our new life together in a new country.

In a physical sport such as boxing one expects plenty of injuries. I can honestly say I've never had any fear about being injured. If I had, I would've had to retire immediately because my opponents would have me beaten psychologically. That's not to say I haven't taken some tough punishment in the ring. But, to me, boxing is not about experiencing physical pain. It is about challenging your body and mind. It is about focusing your mind to ignore any pain.

I am also often asked about the prominent scar on my upper lip. Everyone assumes it was the result of a heavy punch that split my lip. Far from it! It was the result of a simple mistake on my part. In March 1991, just before I was due to go to a special training camp near Moscow, an annoying pimple appeared just above my top lip. In our youth, we've all had them at some time. We squeeze them and they clear up. Not this time. Squeezing had little effect. Indeed, the spot became infected. I awoke on my first morning at the camp and my whole face had swollen into a grotesque mask. I couldn't even see out of my eyes. I was rushed into surgery at the local hospital when doctors realised that all my sinuses had become infected and quickly cut into my face to relieve the pressure of the infection. I found out later that had they delayed for just a couple of hours I could have died. The scar is a constant reminder of how close I went to meeting my Maker.

SCAR

Soviet hopefuls at the 1991 European Championships (left to right) — the 1989 light-middleweight champ Israel Akopkochyan, gold medal winner in the super-heavyweight division at the 1990 Goodwill Games, Yevgeny Belousov, and me

Champion of the world. What could be better than winning the world title in sunny Sydney in 1991?

I show off my gold medal after winning the European Championships in Gothenburg in 1991. Chernya is really happy despite keeping a poker face

What happened to the Sydney sunshine? The icy winter weather in Serov, after I returned as world champion, was a dramatic contrast to that in the country where I was about to make my new home. Chernya and I are well rugged up

The fans braved the cold to greet me on my return to Russia as world champion

RAY CONNELLY

Australia's most famous ring announcer, who was part of Bill Mordey's team involved with my early professional career. The unique ring introductions of the late Ray Connelly were characterised by his wonderful use of alliteration. He was also a highly respected judge of boxing talent. His mates used to call him 'Lord' which was short for Lord of the Ring.

PUNISHING PUGALISTIC PREDISPOSITION

There was a whole group of us at Bill Mordey's home in Coogee when Kostya agreed to come to Australia. Bill called me over and asked: 'Lord, can you give us one of your introductions for Kostya?'

I stood up in front of the dozen or so who were there and did the honours. It went something like this — 'Ladeeez and gentlemennnn! Introducing, in the red corner, from the Siberian city of Serov, the

reeeeemarkable Russian rapier whose punishing pugalistic predisposition, sensational Soviet sporting stamina and fantastic, ferocious flair will ultimately lead him to the world championship…the Prince of Pain…Kostya Tszyuuuuuu.'

Of course, Kostya didn't understand English…he didn't know what I was saying. But he sensed it. He truly sensed it. When I pointed at him and announced his name, he leapt to his feet and threw his arms in the air with his fists clenched. And that cheeky smile of his spread over his face.

Forget about the hours in the gym. Forget about stepping into the ring. At that moment he had become a professional fighter.

But, once in the ring, his wonderful array of talents was all too obvious. Those of us involved with Kostya were blessed. Once in a lifetime you see somebody who will be infinitely great. This was Kostya. He was such a natural. From the day I first saw him fight professionally, I knew he was a monster who was cool and calculated. He was the dux of his class.

One of his great attributes was his ability to lift when required. His controlled aggression, ferocious punching power and amazing eye-hand co-ordination genuinely astounded me. His ability was God-given. I've never seen anyone move so quickly in so many different directions. He had the amazing ability to alter a blow just two or three inches from his target. He was pure talent. Unique.

[Kostya] has the eye of a hawk, the heart of a lion and the strike power of a cobra.

Trainer Johnny Lewis

My first fight was over in a matter of seconds — with the photographers missing out on the action. Johnny Lewis gives me a hug while a delighted Peter Mitrevski runs in from my corner to join us

CROSSED WIRES

I MADE MY PROFESSIONAL DEBUT ON 1 MARCH 1992 in the open air at Princes Park, the home ground of the Carlton Aussie Rules football team in Melbourne. It was a low-key affair. No one took much notice of me, even though I was the reigning world amateur champion. After all, my bout was on the undercard to a much-awaited pro world title fight in which Aussie Jeff Fenech was hoping for revenge against Azumah Nelson of Ghana. Jeff reckoned he had been robbed when their first bout in Las Vegas had been declared a draw. But Jeff lost out in Melbourne.

I found out a couple of years later that my opponent, Darrell Hiles, had been hand-picked by Bill Mordey to ensure I had a relatively easy debut in the pro ranks. Darrell, an Aboriginal fighter from Queensland, was a solid boxer but not expected to make a big impact in the sport. Eleven months earlier Darrell had been chosen for similar reasons when another fighter who had been successful in the amateur ranks made his debut — Grahame 'Spike' Cheney, who had won a silver medal at the Seoul Olympics, beaten on points in the final of the light-welterweight division by my Soviet teammate, the experienced 31-year-old Vyacheslav Yanovsky. Darrell had also been at the Seoul Olympics, where he had been beaten in the second round of clashes in the featherweight division by the eventual bronze medal winner, South Korean Lee Jae-hyuk. In their pro clash Spike had knocked Darrell out for his first and, by the time he met me, only loss in eight bouts.

Bill eventually found a video of one of Darrell's fights and I studied him closely before writing in my diary: 'He's tall, with a good left hook. If it weren't my first professional bout he wouldn't provide any problems. But it will be the first time I have fought over 10 rounds. Ten rounds is a long time.'

On the morning of the fight I wrote a more revealing entry in my diary: 'Another four hours and part of my life's history will have unfolded. Everything is depending on this day. But everything will be fine. I have prepared so well that I cannot fail.'

Apparently Bill had told Johnny to persuade me to treat the fight as just another spar in the gym. He wanted me to have a few rounds so he could get some video to use as publicity on television. But, of course, there was the problem of language. I couldn't speak English and Johnny knew not a word of Russian.

There had been an interpreter to translate Johnny's instructions between rounds but he didn't manage to explain the trainer's final instructions before the bout began. I thought Johnny had told me to win the fight in the opening round. So I did. Boom, boom, boom! Poor Darrell went down in a heap after the first mid-ring confrontation. I knocked him out in less than a minute.

When I got back into the dressing room I got the interpreter to ask Johnny why it was so important to win the fight in the first round.

Johnny just smiled and replied: 'I didn't say that. I told you to make sure you *won* the first round. You had another nine in which to win the fight!'

In the lead-up to my first professional bout, I met boxing great Virgil Hill. Just like me, Virgil was fighting in Melbourne on the undercard to the Jeff Fenech-Azumah Nelson rematch. Virgil was coming off a loss to Thomas 'Hitman' Hearns, who had taken the WBA world light-heavyweight title that Hill had held for the previous two years. Hill was to later regain the title and add an International Boxing Federation world crown to his record. He retired in 2004 after losing the WBA crown in his 54th bout

Preparing for my first pro fight

Johnny Lewis and I are ready for action.

But he was pleased, nevertheless. He told reporters: 'I'll be one very disappointed person if Kostya doesn't win a world title. He has the eye of a hawk, the heart of a lion and the strike power of a cobra. Talk about potential? Kostya Tszyu has the potential to win a world title within 18 months. He's a kid in a million.'

It was a stroke of luck that when I moved to Australia I should join the camp of Johnny Lewis. There has probably never been a greater trainer of Australian boxers than Johnny. At the time I met him in 1991 he had trained two world champions. The first was Jeff Fenech, the bloke the media called 'The Marrickville Mauler'. He was to become one of the greats of boxing, winning world crowns in three different weight divisions. The other Lewis world champion was Jeff 'Hit Man' Harding. I was to become the third.

Johnny had been in the fight game for 30 years. He had learned to fight in 1957 at the age of 13 in the Newtown Police Boys Club in inner Sydney. He was taught by a trainer called Dick O'Connor and never

lost a fight while Dick was in his corner. When Johnny was 17, O'Connor left to look after a member of his family who was ill and never came back. Lewis took over as trainer simply because he was the oldest kid in the squad.

But Johnny was more than just a trainer. He was like a second father to the kids in his care. Not all were boxers. There were many tough rugby league players and, like the boxers, more than a few swore that Johnny's care and attention kept them from turning to crime and a likely life in jail.

Johnny left nothing to chance in the way he prepared me for all my fights, and as history shows he looked after me when I was in the ring just as a father would look after his son.

I had space in our home at
Sans Souci in which to train

HOME SWEET HOME

I HAVE CERTAINLY COME A LONG WAY since those years when I was growing up, with us all living in that one room of the apartment in Serov. Never in my wildest dreams did I ever think that one day I would have my own family and be living in a big house like we do today.

In Serov after years of waiting, we moved to a three-bedroom apartment. And then my skills as a boxer earned me my own apartment. Nothing very grand by Australian standards, but the envy of other Russians.

Then it was off to Sydney to start my professional career.

Looking back, I just shake my head when I think of the first house Natasha and I called home. Bill Mordey had promised to find us a furnished house for the first 12 months. By that time we would have found our feet and could hopefully buy our own home. Bill wanted to put us in an apartment — but we wanted a place where we could have pets. I really wanted a dog. And, to tell the truth, we wanted a house because each of us had lived in apartments all our life and this would be the symbol of our new life together. We wanted a house near a park, a shopping centre and a beach. And we didn't want to be too far from Johnny Lewis' gym. We settled on a place in O'Riordan Street in Mascot. We didn't know it at the time — but we could hardly have made a worse choice. We knew nothing about Mascot, an industrial suburb with the airport slap bang in the middle of it.

At dawn on the first morning in our new home we soon found out. The first of a steady stream of semi-trailers began roaring past the front door, shaking the devil out of the house. And right on 6am, at the end of the overnight curfew on flights in and out of Sydney Airport, the first of the jumbo jets roared overhead. We could hardly hear ourselves think. Natasha and I looked at each other and laughed out loud. Welcome to our new life.

Brian Mills, our unofficial chauffeur and general roustabout, had found furniture. The lounges and beds and refrigerator were leftovers from when he and his girlfriend had decided to move in together. They had two of everything and would have had to get rid of them. They weren't anything like the luxury of the Quay West apartments on Sydney Harbour where we had stayed when we arrived in Australia. But they were better than most families in Russia ever had. Anyway, we didn't care. We had each other and we were very much in love.

Six months later we decided 'Yes, it's too noisy in Mascot' and we wanted to follow 'the great Australian dream' and own our own house. We had been saving every cent we could and my cheque from the fight against Larry LaCoursiere in Newcastle brought the savings to $65,000. Enough for a deposit on a home of our own. We found what we wanted in the suburb of Sans Souci, near Botany Bay. It was big enough for the family we planned and there was also enough room for my Mama and Papa when I brought them out from Russia. And, of course, room for my two dogs, a Rottweiler named Viking (who was with us for a decade, and who, since his death, I have sorely missed) and a small long-haired Tibetan which I named Malishka after my old dog in Serov. I also had a pet Electus parrot named Leha, which sadly flew off one day when frightened by a sudden noise and never came back.

I got to know all the neighbours at Sans Souci. Everyone would stop and ask us how the preparation for the next fight was going and how the family was settling in. Australians are like that.

After almost a decade at Sans Souci we decided to build our dream home at nearby Carss Park. There would be plenty of room for the kids. I would have my own gym, tennis court and

I love all animals of all shapes, sizes and species. Here I am with a couple of my pet parrots. If I look a bit strained it's because they had decided to leave tiny calling cards on my shoulders

Our first baby — Viking as a puppy

I have no fear of snakes, despite what one ill-informed newspaper columnist said about this encounter. This wasn't at home but at Taronga Zoo in Sydney when we were publicising the 2005 Ricky Hatton encounter

swimming pool to help me keep in shape when I was not in full training. There would also be lots of room for our menagerie of pets, including a big aquarium and a reptile enclosure for pet snakes. And there was a nearby park in which I could run, clocking up the roadwork so necessary when preparing for big fights.

When we moved, Mama and Papa were able to take over the whole house at Sans Souci. With that I had been able to achieve one of my lifelong goals of providing for them for the rest of their lives. They had looked after me as a kid. Now it was my turn to look after them.

But no matter what bricks and mortar make up a house … no matter how many rooms it has … no matter whether there is a swimming pool or a gym or a sauna … it is the people who live there that turn a house into a home. And with my darling Natasha and our three kids I have a truly wonderful home, full of love and happiness and dreams of a great future for all of us.

What more could a bloke from Serov ask for!

In the backyard at the Sans Souci home

BRIAN MILLS

A member of the staff of promoter Bill Mordey when I arrived in Sydney to start my professional career. He was our 'chauffeur' and guide in this strange new city. He was the person who found Natasha and me a new home (and furnished it). He taught us all about the weird and wonderful Aussie way of life that confronted us. But, most of all, he became our friend.

AUSSIE DAD

I first met Kostya when he was in Sydney for the 1991 amateur world championships. Trainer Johnny Lewis had seen him in action overseas and had shouted the praises of this smiling, amiable Russian boxer.

'Remember that Russian I told you about, Bill?' Johnny said one day. Bill Mordey nodded. He had almost certainly long forgotten the conversation but wasn't going to let on. 'Well, Bill,' Johnny continued, 'he's fighting tonight and you'd better come and take a look at him.' Bill wasn't about to argue and we all went along to watch this Russian with the unusual pigtail. Johnny wasn't wrong. The kid was dynamite — or more to the point the kid had dynamite in both his fists. Bill ordered us to pull out all stops to ensure Kostya was signed to turn professional and fight under the Mordey banner.

'Let's show him and his entourage some real Aussie hospitality,' Bill said. 'We'll have a barbie at my place. Plenty of seafood and plenty of Stolly [Stolichnaya vodka].' Another of the Mordey crew and I were ordered to keep the Russian officials — a trainer and a doctor, if I recall correctly — happy. Their glasses were regularly topped up with vodka and everything was going swimmingly until Bill's pet cat piddled on the leg of one of the officials. Luckily, he wasn't too fussed — even though Bill was. The long and the short of it was that Kostya agreed to come to live in Australia and start his journey to a professional world title.

Bill appointed me as Kostya and Natasha's minder. Not a bodyguard, but a general roustabout. I met them at the airport when they arrived and drove them to a media conference that had been arranged at Quay West, a luxury block of serviced apartments that overlooked the Harbour Bridge, Opera House and the harbour itself. If you or I wanted to stay there it would cost an arm and a leg. But the general manager, Graham Goldberg, was an old friend and a sports nut who understood the value of publicity — even involving a virtually unknown Russian boxer.

Halfway up the Quay West tower was an opulent indoor swimming pool and one of the television guys thought it would look good to have Kostya diving into the pool and coming up all smiles. He didn't have a swimsuit — but one of the reporters did. Somehow we managed in sign language — none of us spoke Russian and Kostya didn't speak a word of English — to explain what we wanted. Then suddenly a thought struck me. What if he couldn't swim? After all he was from out near Siberia. As the camera whirred, Kostya made a perfect dive into the pool and swam a couple of laps with the ease of a Murray Rose or an Ian Thorpe. Could he swim? Like a fish! Was there anything this kid couldn't do?

The television people wanted more. So we took him to Centrepoint Tower where one of our mates had a fruit shop — and we loaded him and Natasha up with fresh fruit. Then it was across to David Jones food hall and the cameraman had a field day as Kostya's eyes lit up as they took in the rows and rows of lobsters and huge steaks.

The two of them eventually looked over a house in the suburb of Mascot and decided it was what they wanted — even though it was on the main drag to the airport, with trucks roaring past the front door all day and night. My girlfriend and I had just moved in together and so had plenty of furniture left over which we used to furnish the house. They were like two lovebirds. It was wonderful to see the relationship.

But it was handy to Johnny Lewis' gym. I would drive Kostya to the gym and home again each day. And then he and Natasha enrolled in English classes at Bondi Junction. I've got five kids of my own — and it was like schooldays all over again. I would pick them up at 9am and drive them to their classes and come back at 3pm to drive them home.

I would talk to them in English even though at first they couldn't understand a word. But Natasha told me much later it was a wonderful feeling when she listened to me.

'You were always smiling, you were obviously very happy,' she said. 'You were a real darling.' She called me her 'Aussie Dad' and I felt like a surrogate father to both of them.

Eventually Kostya got his driver's licence and a car and I was no longer needed to ferry them hither and thither. But we were still part of the family. I remember when they moved house to Sans Souci and Kostya's Mum and Dad came out from Russia, Kostya and Natasha threw a party. Bill was a bit worried. At the best of times he ate sparingly and what little he ate was usually pretty plain. Steaks, chops or lobster was the usual fare on the Mordey menu. And I wasn't adventurous in my tastes either. We got the ring announcer Ray Connelly to be our 'taster' — he loved his tucker and would try anything. At the party Ray would look at a dish, give it a try and either nod or shake his head at us. Bill was dying for a bourbon — but everyone was drinking vodka as if there was no tomorrow.

Sadly, Kostya and Bill eventually split. And the split was a bitter one. But there was no animosity between Kostya, Natasha and me. Although these days we live in different parts of Australia and rarely get to see each other, there will always be a special bond between us. A bond going back to those days when neither party could understand the other, but we were firm friends nevertheless.

I had some great sparring partners over the years. One of the best was American Stevie Johnston from Denver, Colorado, who helped me prepare for a couple of my fights. Stevie gave me a torrid time when sparring in the ring. It was obvious he was a champion in the making, so it hardly surprised me that in March 1997, two years after I won my first world title, Stevie beat Frenchman Jean Baptiste Mendy in Paris to win the WBC world lightweight crown. He finally lost the title in 2000 and retired three years later with 35 wins from 39 bouts. In this photo, taken at Leo Berry's gym in the Melbourne suburb of Richmond, I'm with Johnny Lewis, Stevie, my first 'Aussie mate' Brian Mills and Stevie's renowned American trainer Scott Ardrey

LaPorte catches me with a left to the jaw

Making a Name For Myself

I KNEW VIRTUALLY NOTHING ABOUT my second opponent, Ned Simmonds — only that he was a Jamaican-born boxer who lived in the Canadian city of Toronto. And I didn't find out much more about him in the ring. I hit him with a perfect punch in the first round, he went down for the count and never got back on his feet. Next on the knockout list was West Australian Tony Jones. This fight actually went into the second round before … boom, boom, boom … goodbye, Tony.

It was then that Bill and Johnny reckoned it was time for me to meet an opponent worthy of a man with his eyes on a future world crown. They chose a hardened old campaigner named Juan LaPorte. He was a former WBC world featherweight champion who had fought no less than nine world title bouts including one in Sydney against Jeff Fenech's conqueror Azumah Nelson. My fight with him was on the eve of the 1992 Barcelona Olympics — and the media kept asking me whether I was disappointed that I wouldn't be going for gold in Spain.

My first real challenge. Off to the ring with Johnny Lewis to take on Juan LaPorte, the former world champion (in three different weight divisions), in only my fourth professional bout

A talk with Australia's triple world champion Jeff Fenech in Bangkok in 1989 sowed the seeds in my mind for the eventual move to Australia. After the weigh-in for the fight against Sammy Fuentes in Melbourne I needed to instantly build up the carbohydrates, so Jeff and future Australian lightweight champion Justin Rowsell, who was making his pro debut on the same night, encouraged me to demolish a massive plate of pasta

'Beating Juan LaPorte will be my Olympic gold medal,' I told them. The media also questioned the wisdom of going in against such a seasoned campaigner, with a total of 398 rounds in his 15-year career. I had experienced all of 5 minutes and 23 seconds in my three pro fights. Bill Mordey explained the facts of life to the reporters: 'What else could I do? The kid was demolishing well-credentialled fighters. I had to find someone who could stay on his feet.'

After I caught LaPorte with some solid punches in the second round I knew I would win — especially as I expected him to tire in the final rounds. He did and I chalked up a win on points. Just as important was the fact that I had been able to go 10 rounds. In hindsight, it was probably stupid to have gone in against such a fighter when I had such limited professional experience. But I had no fear. Like all young men, I felt I was invincible.

On my way to victory over LaPorte

A first for Fuentas. He had never been knocked out before … and it only took 54 seconds for me to do it

About six weeks later I took on Daniel Cusato, an Argentinian with an awkward fighting style. I had a bit of trouble adapting until, in the seventh round, I blasted him with a crisp uppercut and down he went. Next cab off the rank was Puerto Rican Sammy Fuentes. I didn't know anything about him — but it didn't matter. Slap, bang, wallop … it was all over in 54 seconds. It was the first time in his career that Fuentes had been knocked out. One of the journalists replayed the video of the fight and wrote how I had landed 15 heavy blows to Sammy's head and body in that short space of time — and that didn't include the many jabs setting up the Puerto Rican for the big punches that took their toll. Bill Mordey was all smiles as he told the assembled media: 'The kid's a mini-Mike Tyson.'

It was time to venture overseas — my first international bout as a professional. If I was going to get a chance to fight for the world title I would have to be known in the United States where every one of the top names in my division fought. So it was off to Memphis, Tennessee. My opponent was Steve Larrimore from the Bahamas, a former British Commonwealth champion. He had been told I was very slow and was shocked at my speed. So shocked that I was able to put him away in the second round!

63

After the Fuentas fight. His face says it all

Back in Australia I had my first fight in Newcastle, a city I grew to love so much that it seemed like a second home to me. I took on Larry LaCoursiere, an American from the state of Minnesota. He boasted a good record. But that suffered a real setback in Newcastle. I hit him with a flurry of punches, notably a right uppercut, a straight left and a left uppercut, and the fight was all over in the first round. A month later I was back in Newcastle to fight another American, Robert Rivera. The fight lasted just 87 seconds as Rivera went down in a crumpled heap. I felt I was cheating the Newcastle fans, even though they didn't seem to mind as they cheered their lungs out. I was happy that my next opponent in the steel city was a former WBA world lightweight champion, Livingston Bramble. Perhaps this time I could give the Novocastrians a bit more for their money. It was the first time I had come across one of those American fighters who are liberal with their boasts. At the media conferences you couldn't shut him up. And, quite frankly, neither could I in the ring. He was a tough fighter who refused to go down, even though he spent most of the fight retreating from my barrage of punches. At the end of the scheduled 10 rounds I was named the winner on points.

My record now stood at 10 fights for 10 wins. Only two of the bouts had gone the 10 rounds. All the rest were either knockouts or TKOs where the referee stopped the fight.

'The kid was demolishing well-credentialled fighters. I had to find someone who could stay on his feet.'

Promoter Bill Mordey

With Livingston Bramble after our fight in Newcastle. He was a real crowd-pleaser both with his 100 percent effort and outrageous spiky hair

STUART ROACH

A respected newspaper columnist and former sporting editor of the Newcastle Herald, Roach covered all of my fights in Newcastle, including the first world title bout ever staged in that industrial city.

LOCAL HERO

Newcastle and the coalfields of the Hunter Valley have a proud boxing heritage. They were the home to Les Darcy, the man everyone thought would win Australia's first universally recognised world title — but who ended his life amid controversy over whether he had shirked duty in World War I. More than 100,000 fans turned up for his funeral at Maitland, in the coalfields on 1 July 1917.

Then there was Dave Sands, who life was so cruelly snuffed out in a motor accident in 1952 just as a world crown was there for the taking. After all, he had beaten all the leading contenders except Randy Turpin who pulled out of a fight with Sands to take on the legendary Sugar Ray Robinson for the world middleweight championship in an era when there was only one title, not like the many so-called world crowns of today.

So it was perhaps predictable that the people of Newcastle should open their arms to a man who would become one of the greatest world champions of all time — Kostya Tszyu. So what if he wasn't from the coalfields. So what that when he stepped into the ring at the Newcastle Entertainment Centre for the first time his English vocabulary was restricted to a few basic phrases. G'day. Thank you. I love Newcastle.

And the people of Newcastle loved Kostya Tszyu. He repaid them by appearing in more professional fights in Newcastle than in any other city that had been lucky enough to play host to this wonderful fighter. He fought six times in Sydney, on five occasions in Las Vegas and had four fights in Melbourne. But he punched his way to victory seven times in Newcastle.

Okay, so some of his appearances were pretty brief.

The first time was back on 14 May 1993. Kostya arrived with a record of seven victories in as many bouts — all but one inside the distance. He quickly won the hearts of the fans with his trademark entrance, vaulting over the top ring rope. The introductory fanfare and anthems took about eight minutes. But Tszyu needed only 2 minutes and 42 seconds to lay American Larry LaCoursiere cold on the canvas. The crowd of 3500 loved it. They didn't feel robbed by the quick finish to the fight. They were delirious, shouting the house down. 'Kostya, Kostya, Kostya.' They had a new hero. And in hard economic times they certainly needed one.

A month later the stadium was packed again. Not only did those fans who had watched the one-round demolition of LaCoursiere return, but they brought many of their mates with them. This time the slaughter was even more complete. Kostya floored another American, Robert Rivera, after 40 seconds. He got to his feet jelly-legged and Kostya finished him off with a vicious right to the jaw in the 87th second.

Two fights that had not even lasted a round each. One would have thought the two quick demolitions would have been bad for ticket sales in any future promotion. Hardly! In halting English, Tszyu told the people of Newcastle that the smokestacks so characteristic of the city's industry reminded him of his home city of Serov. Les Darcy or Dave Sands could not have expected the warmth of the fans' response.

Tszyu visited the BHP steelworks, now so sadly closed down, before he took on former WBA world champion Livingston Bramble in his next Newcastle fight. The BHP riggers became honorary members of the family for his visit, taping imitation rat's tails to the back of their safety helmets to imitate Kostya's unique hairstyle. This time they saw a bit more action. He went the full 12 rounds with Bramble. When he won he promised the fans that when (and not if) he won the world championship he would defend his title in Newcastle.

They knew he wouldn't disappoint them. After a sidetrack to the Florida Everglades, where he beat Hector Lopez, he returned for yet another fight on his methodical journey to world championship status. When he beat Angel Hernandez in a seventh-round TKO in May 1994, local radio station 2HD broadcast the fight to listeners in the Hunter Valley. It was the first fight broadcast on local radio in 40 years. The stadium was packed to the rafters. The radio ratings soared.

Just over a year later Kostya fulfilled his promise. Back from America where he had surprised the Yanks by taking out Jake 'The Snake' Rodriguez to win the IBF junior-welterweight championship, Kostya made his first title defence in the steel city, against another American, Roger Mayweather. The following year after a couple of fights in Sydney he was back in town to beat South African Jan Piet Bergman.

'I love fighting here,' he said.

He would do so only one more time, demolishing Calvin Grove in three rounds in 1997 as he was on the road back after the first (and at that time only) loss of his career. Since then the television moguls have decided it's not economically feasible for a fight in Newcastle. So we in the steel city now live with just the memories of our adopted son, Kostya Tszyu, and the way he won the hearts of those of us in the Hunter.

WEDDING BELLS

IN SEPTEMBER 1993, I took Natasha home to Serov for a long-awaited holiday. And I had a real surprise for her once we got home. I would ask her to marry me. Once she was reunited with her family the tears flowed. But not as much as when I unveiled my big surprise. We were all sitting around when I suddenly asked her parents for their permission for me to marry her. Natasha's Mama turned to her and asked why she hadn't told her about this beforehand.

'How could I, Mama,' Natasha blurted out. 'It's the first I have heard about it.' She didn't have to be asked. Natasha just turned to me and said: 'Yes, Kostya, yes, yes, yes.'

I was bold enough to assume the answers from Natasha and her parents would be positive, so I had already made all the arrangements. The wedding was set down for the following Saturday — 24 September. I had slipped quietly away and filled out all the official documents and I had found a wonderful restaurant for the wedding reception. It was a real rush for Natasha to find the wedding clothes. Her Mama found a seamstress who quickly made a simple, but beautiful wedding gown. And Natasha arranged for some lovely shoes to be sent from Moscow. There was a bit of a hiccup when the shoes arrived and they were a size too small. Under Russian tradition the groom must place the shoes on the bride's feet, in the style of Cinderella and her Prince Charming. Somehow I managed this at the wedding. Natasha told me afterwards how much her feet hurt — but she couldn't care less. Nothing could ever spoil our big day.

There was another Russian tradition in which I had to meet all the neighbours and answer their questions about Natasha. Australians may find this amusing. I had to get a lot of questions right to show I knew enough about her to be a worthy husband. On the other hand, I had to purposely give plenty of wrong answers to show I didn't know too much. And with each wrong answer I had to give the person who had posed the question a present. Tradition demands the groom has to give away lots and lots of presents.

The one last tradition is that the happy couple immediately set about starting a family. This we duly did — and, back in Australia, four months later Natasha's doctor confirmed the good news. She was pregnant. Another generation of the Tszyu family was about to begin.

Back home after another success in 2002 ... time to await the birth of Anastasia

My first appearance on United States television proved to be the toughest fight of my short career. It was against Mexican Hector Lopez at Tampa in Florida. After three fine rounds, for some inexplicable reason I suddenly became fatigued and had difficulty keeping my fists up in front of me. But as Lopez fought his way back into the fight Johnny Lewis kept reassuring me. And as swiftly as it appeared the fatigue vanished and I won the final three rounds to take the judges' decision on points.

Then it was back to Newcastle for a match that coincided with the Russian Orthodox Easter. I took on a clever Puerto Rican, Angel Hernandez, who was much taller than me. But I had his measure and when he suffered a bad gash to his forehead in the seventh round, the referee was forced to stop the bout and crown me the winner.

Up close and personal against Angel Hernandez in Newcastle

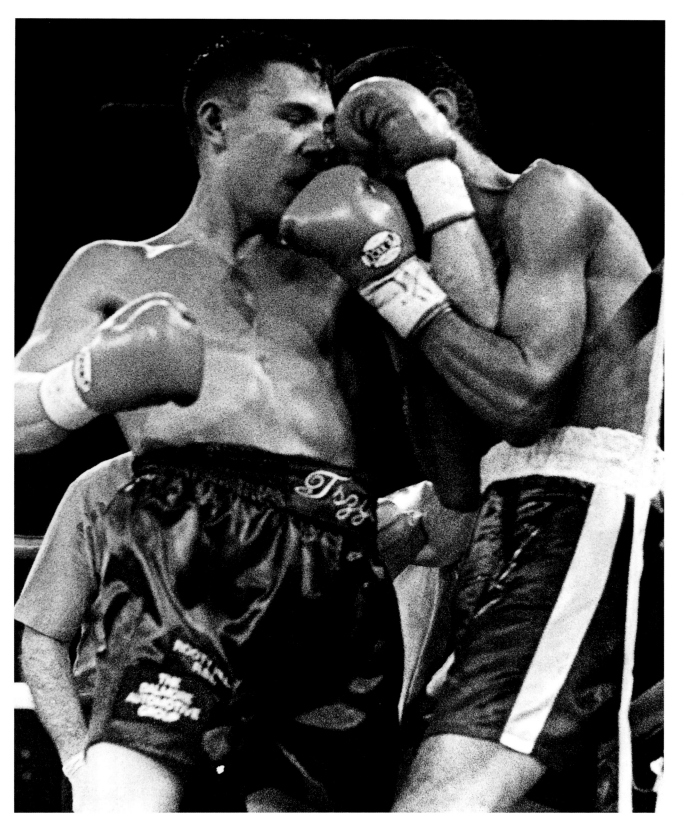

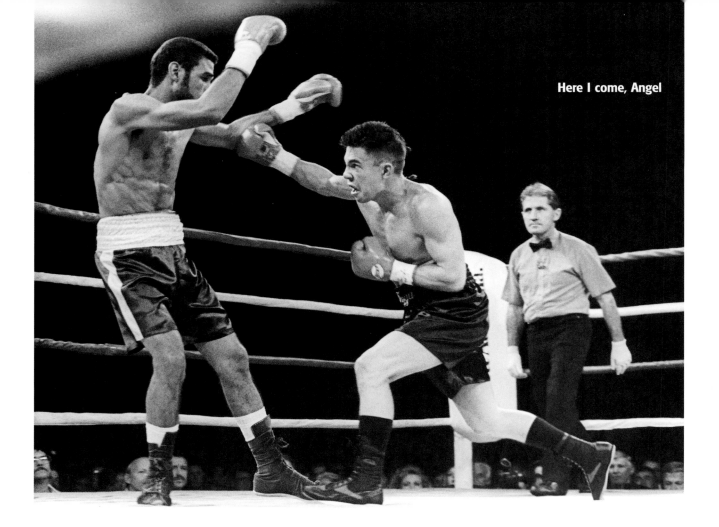

Here I come, Angel

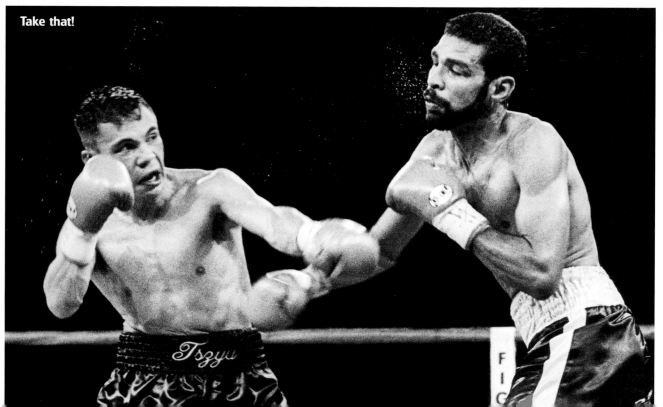

Take that!

I went into my next fight, in Melbourne against Pedro Sanchez of the Dominican Republic, carrying injuries to both hands and my left shoulder. But, as I did in so many of my title defences, I kept them secret. Sanchez was known as 'Toro Loco' (The Mad Bull). But like an expert matador I deceived him with my artistry. The referee stopped the fight in the fourth round.

'Toro Loco' is tamed

The end is near for Jake the Snake

MY DREAM REALISED

MY DATE WITH DESTINY HAD ARRIVED — 28 January 1995. I challenged Jake 'The Snake' Rodriguez for the IBF world junior-welterweight champion at the MGM Grand Casino in Las Vegas. I realised all along that I needed to be in my best form, even though for the first time in my professional career I was going into a fight without an injury of some type. Jake had lost only two fights during his career. And one of those losses was to the great fellow Puerto Rican Felix Trinidad, winner of four world titles in three different weight divisions.

Jake was tough. I had to chase him all the way and he took everything I threw at him, blows from every direction. Jab, jab, jab! Punch, punch, punch! I eventually sent him down to the canvas twice in the fifth round. And I knocked him down another three times in Round Six before the ref stepped in and stopped the fight. A check of the video of the fight showed I had thrown 410 punches in almost 17 minutes in the ring and 168 had cleanly found their mark.

Johnny Lewis told the media: 'I think to beat a champion in the way he did speaks volumes for the ability of Kostya. When you're a champion, you know you're the best. That's what Kostya is. But he's going to improve. Kostya is going to be a super-duper fighter. Certainly I think he will become the best fighter pound-for-pound in the entire world.'

‘Kostya is going to be a super-duper fighter. Certainly I think he will become the best fighter pound-for-pound in the entire world.’

Johnny Lewis

I'm on top of the world. Johnny Lewis lifts me into the air in triumph

And how's this for a celebration cake? They're the only type of gloves I enjoy tasting

I don't know who was more excited about me winning my first professional world title, me or Papa. Here he is in our Las Vegas hotel wearing a T-shirt featuring me in action with the world title belt taken from Jake Rodriguez draped across his body. It's a case of V for Victory

On 19 May 1995, in a quiet ceremony at Rockdale Town Hall near our home in Sans Souci, we joined half a dozen other 'new Australians' to pledge our allegiance to our new country — thus joining our son Timophey who had become an Australian citizen at birth

My world championship victory over Jake Rodriguez meant I could get rid of my old car and go upmarket. A brand-new Lexus Tszyu

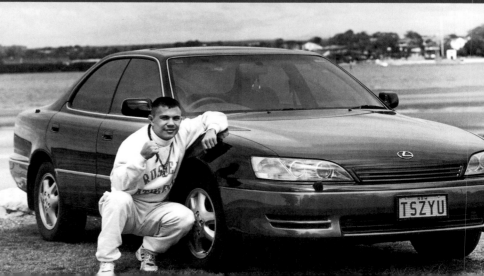

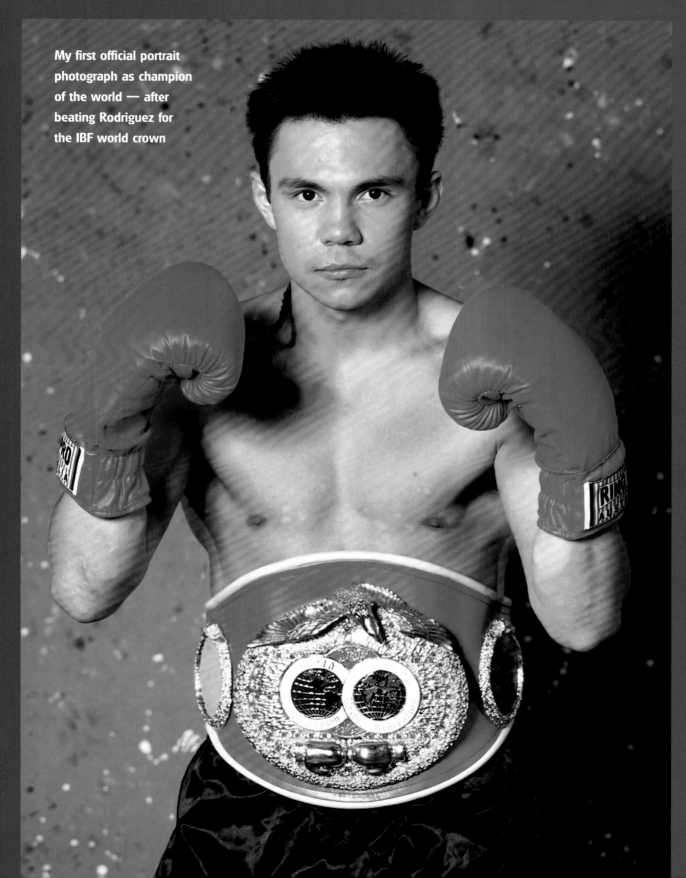

My first official portrait photograph as champion of the world — after beating Rodriguez for the IBF world crown

ANGELO DUNDEE

One of the most respected trainers in the history of boxing. He is credited as being the brains behind the rise to legendary status of arguably the greatest world heavyweight boxing champion of all time, Muhammad Ali.

AGGRESSION PERSONIFIED

Kostya Tszyu is so sharp and he's so ready to fight. Kostya has his own distinctive style. The way he floats with his left hand is an interesting thing. He mesmerises you with it. Then 'bing', he'll hit you with it.

He is aggression personified. He grinds opponents into the ground. His form of aggression is not something that is casual. Every time he comes at you, he's looking to hit you with a certain punch; it could be a leading right hand, a sucker jab or a body punch. He's a good body puncher. He'll fight all day long.

If you fight Kostya Tszyu, you've got to be ready for a 15-round fight and be full of aggression. You also have to be 150 percent better than what you are normally – otherwise you won't live with Kostya Tszyu.

Kostya is so pretty to see when he throws his punches. Everything is a precision punch, then, when he hits you up close with a body shot, he's just tremendous.

He can knock you out with either hand.

To me, Kostya Tszyu is a great champion.

'If you fight Kostya Tszyu, you've got to be ready for a 15-round fight and be full of aggression.'

Angelo Dundee

JIM GESTAKOVSKI

Macedonian-born Sydney real estate agent who breeds Rottweilers as a hobby. After selling Natasha and me a puppy we called Viking, Jim became a great mate. He and his wife Vera are probably our closest friends in Australia.

SHOULD HAVE BEEN A PRIEST

My wife and I met Kostya and Natasha only a couple of weeks after they arrived in Australia. So I suppose you could say we are the only ones who have been with them continuously from the very start in their new country. They bought a Rottweiler puppy off us. And as I spoke a bit of Russian it was quite natural for Vera and me to try to help these 'new Australians'. Tell me about it … I knew exactly what they were going through as I had come to Australia in 1965 and speaking not a word of English at the time found it a real culture shock. I knew all the pitfalls that awaited them.

   Kostya eventually began joining my friends and me on excursions. We'd go on fishing trips, hunting or camping. And from Day One, on a shooting trip near the famous old gold-mining town of Sofala, west of the Blue Mountains, he always did his fair share of the work … and more.

Just one of the boys. On a fishing trip with 'Team Gestakovski' at Yass in southern NSW, 1999

Natasha and Tim with our 'second Mum and Dad' — Jimmy and Vera Gestakovski

Vera and I 'adopted' Kostya as our son. After all, we didn't have a son of our own, just two lovely daughters, Susie and Lily. Kostya and Natasha's children are like grandchildren to us. I remember when Tim was born. Long into the night Kostya and I toasted the birth with glass after glass of vodka. Indeed, too many glasses of vodka for our own good!

Vera and I have seen about half of his fights live. The rest we have watched on PayTV. And we could not have been more proud had it been our own flesh and blood in the ring. But then again all Australians are proud of Kostya. Why? Well, personally I can vouch for the fact that he is a very nice person. He is also a wonderful friend who would give his life for you if he likes you. That's why I love him.

In real life Kostya wouldn't hurt a fly. He told me after some of his victories that he felt sorry for his opponents. 'But a job is a job, Jimmy,' he would add. I'd shake my head and tell him: 'Kostya, you should have been a priest.' And he would laugh.

You know, every day I love him more. In the ring, he is a champion. Out of the ring, he is also a champion.

Jim and Tim in 1997 — the next champion Tszyu gives 'adopted' grandfather Jimmy Gestakovski a few boxing tips

JOHNNY LEWIS

The greatest trainer in the history of Australian boxing. When I first met him he had already schooled two world champions from his gym in the Sydney suburb of Newtown. Jeff Fenech had won world titles in three different weight divisions (IBF bantamweight, WBC super-bantamweight and WBC featherweight) and Jeff 'Hit Man' Harding had been WBC world light-heavyweight champ. Johnny was also involved with several top rugby league sides including the Australian Test team.

INCREDIBLE MENTAL TOUGHNESS

I would say my greatest asset as a boxing trainer is that I genuinely care for my blokes. Not just in the ring but outside as well. Money is not important. The greatest reward is after a fight when a young bloke puts his arms around me and says, 'Thanks, Johnny.' And you know he means it.

It's always been that way with Kostya.

I had first noticed him at the Moscow world championships in 1989. If you had asked me at the time whether he won or lost, I couldn't have answered. All I know he was a standout … a winner even if he didn't end up with the gold medal. There was something about him — something I couldn't put my finger on. All I knew was that he had the potential to become one of the greatest boxers of all time if he were to embark on a professional career.

What attracted my attention? I can't really say. I suppose it's like when [Brisbane Broncos rugby league coach] Wayne Bennett sees a kid with talent playing football in some remote country town or when [horseracing trainer] Bart Cummings sees a horse enter the sale ring. They know … they just know. So it was with Kostya. I told [Sydney promoter] Bill Mordey about him. And the die was cast.

After Kostya's first professional fight, in Melbourne, I told the media: 'I'll be one very disappointed person if Kostya doesn't win a world title. He has the eye of a hawk, the heart of a lion and the strike power of a cobra. Talk about potential? Kostya Tszyu has the potential to win a world title within 18 months. He's a kid in a million.' And I never deviated from that opinion.

Kostya has always had so much going for him. His punches were explosive. He had an incredible hand speed. He knew no fear and he had an abundance of natural talent. But what set him apart from all the other thousands of would-be champions was his mental approach.

I have never known an athlete in any chosen sport, anywhere in the world, who was more focused than Kostya in what he was trying to achieve. The mental side to Kostya has been unbelievable. I suppose it probably has a lot to do with his background and the fact that he had so many amateur fights. It has all been regimented in his mind. He has always had this amazing ability to become focused on the immediate job on hand and leave absolutely nothing to chance. This incredible mental toughness and focus made him the greatest junior-welterweight of all time. I wouldn't have swapped Kostya for anyone.

How ironic! Bill and I sit in front of an advertisement for Ansett Australia.
The airline subsequently went broke and Bill and I split up

A BITTER SPLIT

MY RELATIONSHIP WITH PROMOTER BILL MORDEY has been the subject of much speculation over the years. An ex-journalist, Bill was popular with the media. They dubbed him 'Break-Even Bill' because his stock answer, when asked if he had made a profit from a fight he promoted, was: 'Just broke even, mate!' After our split, some of Bill's friends painted me in a bad light in the pages of their newspapers.

Immediately after my move to Australia he had been like a big brother to me — an integral part of my Aussie 'family'. After all, had it not been for Bill I would never have come to live in Australia. He and his team helped us over many of our early problems. He sent Natasha and me to special English classes to learn the new language. And his team found us a place to live and furniture to put in it.

After taking the world title from Jake Rodriguez, my Aussie 'family' fell apart. There were bitter recriminations and, like in some messy divorce cases, it all ended up in court.

The breakup came quickly. I threw a celebration party after the victory in Las Vegas — but Bill didn't turn up. He had been angry about the involvement of a Russian friend from Sydney, Vlad Warton, in my financial affairs, particularly as Vlad had suggested I have my contract rewritten. Then my hotel room was robbed and there were angry words exchanged when I found Bill did not have insurance cover. In the words of the English expression, the straw that broke the camel's back was a letter that Bill had handed me on our way to Las Vegas. I had taken no notice of it — just throwing it in my suitcase. But when I opened the envelope I received the shock of my life. Bill was advising me he was taking up a two-year option on my contract and had enclosed a cheque for one dollar to enforce the option. I had not even realised there was an option on the contract — and there was to be a great deal of legal argument later about the Russian translation of the agreement.

I knew that what had been mutual trust between us was no longer there and decided to end our relationship once I returned to

Sydney. I would have Vlad as both my manager and promoter. He had no experience as a promoter but would have to learn quickly.

The newspapers were full of quotes from Bill about how I had stabbed him in the back. Most of the journalists wouldn't listen to my side of the story. I recognised I would have to prove myself again in their eyes. And the way to do it was to perform well in the ring and carry myself with dignity outside it.

The court case came at the worst possible time — while I was preparing for what I knew would be a tough world title defence in 1997 against American Vince 'Cool' Phillips in Atlantic City eight weeks later. I had to be in court all day trying to stay mentally alert and then rush off to the gym to put my body through gruelling physical workouts.

Bill was demanding $10 million in damages from me, Vlad, Jeff Fenech, businessman Theo Oinsforou (who had dealt with Vlad) and Sky Channel. I couldn't focus properly on the fight because I was worrying what would happen if by some chance I lost. My lawyers told me I should win, but show me a lawyer who doesn't tell his client that. After 13 days in the NSW Supreme Court the case was over — but Justice Bainton would not give his decision for almost a year.

As history shows, the case took its toll and I was to lose both in the ring and out. I lost to Phillips and subsequently I lost to Mordey. I was training in Newcastle for a fight against Calvin Grove as I battled to get another world title shot when Justice Bainton handed down his decision — a ruling that absolutely shocked me. He ordered me to pay Bill around $7.3 million. The judge called me a spoiled brat which couldn't have been further from the truth as I had always been taught to treat others with the utmost respect, especially my elders. I think the judge based his opinion on some clashes I had with Bill's barrister when I was being cross-examined. He was picking me up on certain nuances in English words that I didn't really understand and I was understandably angry about this. I was left to carry the can after the case against the others was dismissed. I lost my appeal, but the appeal judges implicated Sky Channel which meant we shared the damages. It was still a lot of

I pay my last respects to 'Break-Even' Bill Mordey, chatting with fellow mourners outside Sydney's St Mary's Cathedral after his funeral service in April 2004

money and it would be several years before I could start making money for myself and my family again.

Since then people have often asked what I feel about Bill. Our split cost me a lode of money. But I certainly didn't hate him. Hatred only harms you mentally. Looking back I realise that the break with Bill Mordey was inevitable. But I also know I went about it the wrong way. I feel guilty that I upset Bill. And I feel guilty that I upset the relationship between Bill and Johnny Lewis (they never spoke again). However, I never have and still don't feel guilty about making the break.

A few years later, I felt it was time to rebuild the bridge between Bill and me. I called him on the phone and we made arrangements to meet. I apologised to Bill, not for what I had done but the way I went about it. Over dinner we shared a lot of laughs about old times and at the end it was as if nothing had ever happened. Soon after our reconciliation Bill was diagnosed with terminal cancer, so the timing of our get-together proved to be important. I wouldn't have wanted to carry the burden of our split for the rest of my life. Bill's funeral was an incredible show of affection from all those in the boxing industry. And I said goodbye to a true friend … a man who changed my life forever.

Bill Mordey and his two greatest fighters, Jeff Fenech and me

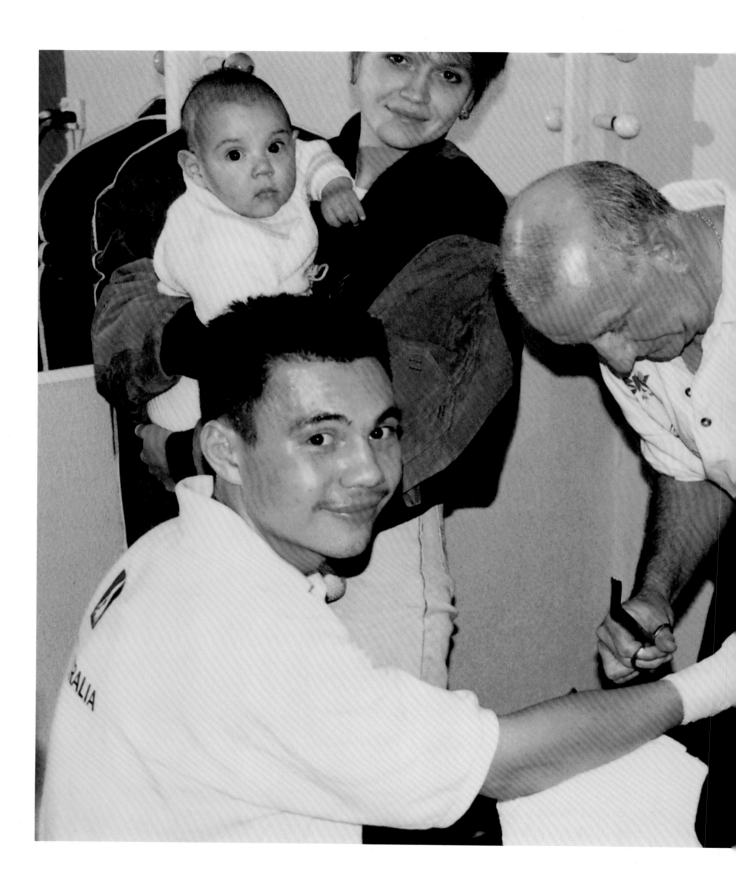

ROUGH RULES IN VEGAS

UNDER MY NEW MANAGEMENT I fought a series of bouts defending my world crown. I had been offered a lot of money to have my first bout in the United States but I preferred to be on familiar territory. Anyway, I had promised the people of Newcastle I would stage a world title bout in the steel city because of their tremendous support. I took on American Roger Mayweather. The press gave him the nickname 'The Black Mamba' after the feared African snake said to be among the fastest and most aggressive of all venomous reptiles. He certainly wasn't as fast as the real-life mamba, relying on spoiling tactics in the ring. And I was battered and bruised at the end — largely thanks to frequent head clashes. Although I couldn't put him away for the count, I posted an easy points victory, with one judge saying I won all but one round and the others giving two rounds to the American.

91

Johnny Lewis is taping my hands in preparation for the Mayweather bout while Tim and Natasha look on

My next challenger, Hugo Pineda, wanted me to stage the defence in a wild city in his native Colombia, noted for its unrest. If it wasn't the drug barons waging their private wars there were riots by groups opposed to the Government. No thanks! After a series of legal battles in court we staged it in the open air at Parramatta Stadium, in Sydney's west. A couple of hours before the fight, Sydney was lashed by an incredible thunderstorm and the 11,000 fans were drenched. Pineda was a tough opponent who refused to give up despite me knocking him down a couple of times. In the end the referee stopped the bout in the 11th round and crowned me the winner. Johnny Lewis told reporters: 'Some of Kostya's right hands would have stopped a buffalo. It's surprising how Pineda survived as long as he did.'

I go on the attack

**Searching for a
way through
Pineda's defences**

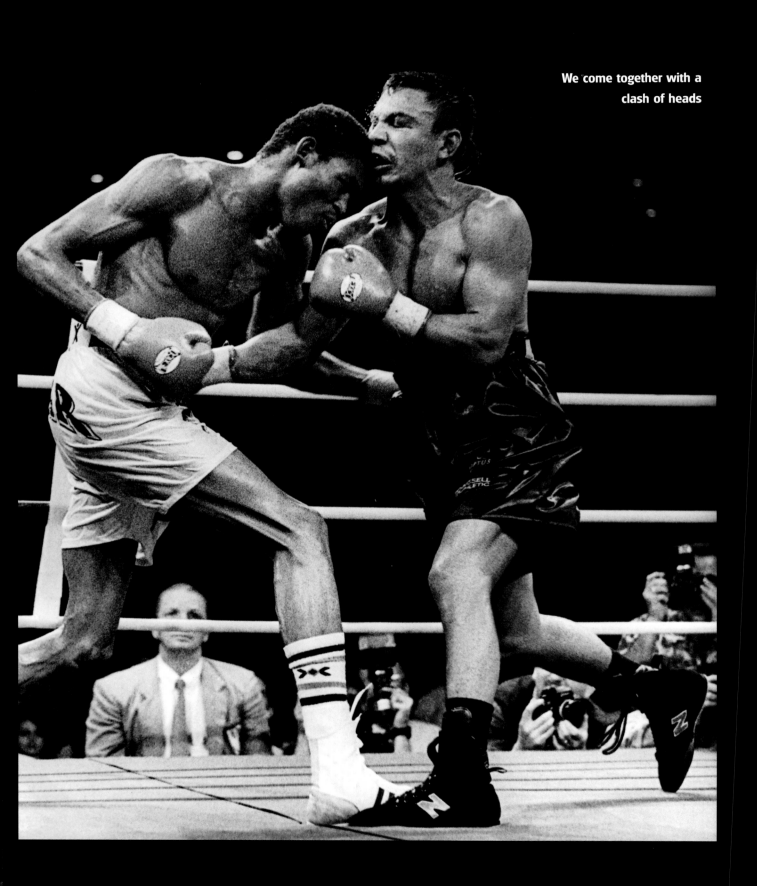

We come together with a
clash of heads

I miss with a right

Pineda thinks he's found an opening

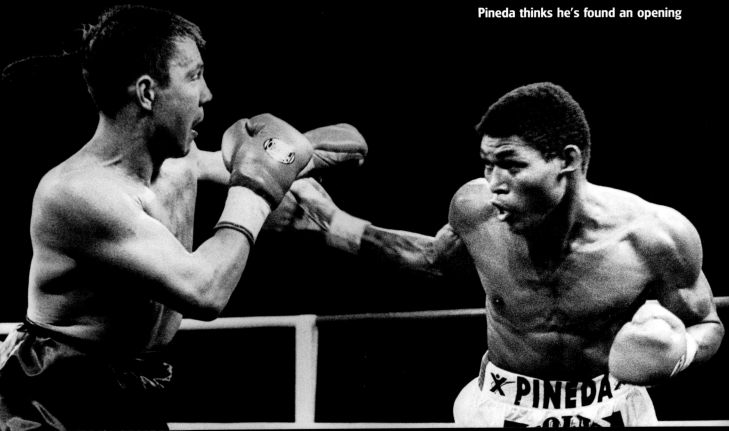

I certainly have

I get through Pineda's defences

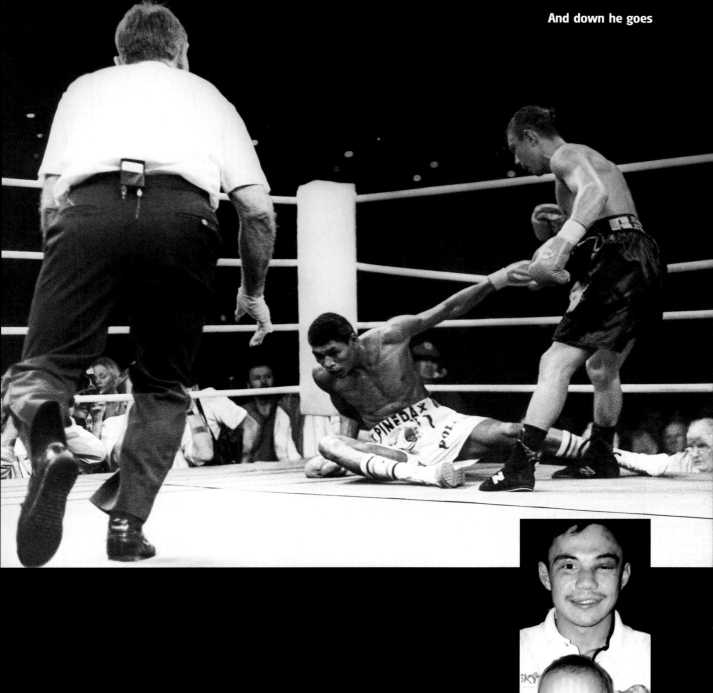

And down he goes

With Tim, the day after my fight with Colombian Hugo Pineda.
I ended up with a black eye. But you should have seen Hugo

American Corey Johnson was next to step into the ring against me, this time at the Sydney Entertainment Centre. I stopped him in four rounds. But he was still a very rugged fighter and I used him as a sparring partner on a couple of occasions later on.

South African Jan Piet Bergman had been ringside to watch the Pineda fight as he was the Number 1 contender and was slated for my first mandatory defence of the IBF crown. We shaped up against each other in Newcastle. In the sixth round there was a clash of heads and I was left with a gaping wound under my left eye. I didn't think they would stop the fight because of this cut, but to make sure of victory I decided to go for broke. He went down once and when he got to his feet I hit him again and he slid out of the ring into a television monitor. The referee, Billy Males, said after the fight: 'Kostya hit him so hard, Bergman was unconscious before he was halfway to the floor.'

For my fourth defence of the world title we went back to Las Vegas to take on Puerto Rican Leonardo Mas. He was a mystery man — as some of the bouts we knew he had fought didn't appear on his CV. And no one really knew just how old he was. The fight had a controversial finish. I thrashed him from pillar to post in the first round and it looked as if his jaw had been broken when the ring doctor called a halt to the fight. But instead of crowning me the winner the referee ruled the match was a technical draw. He alleged I had hit Mas with an unintentional foul blow after he called on us to break. Even the American critics ringside shook their heads in disbelief. But at least I didn't lose my title.

I easily avoid a right-hander from Corey Johnson before putting him away in the fourth round

'Kostya's a beast. In the ring he comes at you like an animal on the prowl wanting to savage you.'

legendary boxer Oscar de la Hoya, who won world titles in five different weight divisions

Is this bloke big … or is gigantic a better description? He makes me look like a jockey. Russian heavyweight Nikolai Valyev (posing with promoter Vlad Warton and me) trained with me in Sydney in 1997. He fought at Bankstown and Parramatta and on the undercard at Atlantic City on the night I went in against Vince Phillips. Valyev now lives in Germany and, by 2005, had fought 41 times without a loss, winning 31 of the bouts by knockout. He stands 2.13m (that's 7ft in the old Imperial measure) and weighs 148kg (23st 3lb)

Referee Benji Estenes moves in to stop my fight with Vince 'Cool' Phillips. That night at the Taj Mahal
Casino Resort in Atlantic City on 31 May 1997 was the lowest point of my life. The bookmakers had
Phillips a 20-1 outsider in our fight. They were ludicrous odds and Johnny Lewis had warned me
about complacency. My preparation had been messed around by the court case with Bill Mordey.
I had focused on that instead of the task ahead of me. And I had made a few mistakes with my diet

ROCK BOTTOM

EARLY EVERYTHING WAS LOOKING GOOD as I took the fight to Vince, jabbing effectively and throwing plenty of hard rights. By the seventh round I felt I had a clear lead. But then something strange happened. I began feeling pain. It was something I had never experienced before. I was often tired in fights, but I was always able to mentally shut out any pain.

In the seventh round, a right from Phillips to my left eye knocked me to the canvas. Only once before had I been knocked off my feet. I was at a loss to realise how it happened. His punches were hurting and I was unable to counter them. Near the end of the ninth round one of my punches opened a huge cut beside his right eye. It almost brought an end to the fight and if it had I would have retained my world title. But the ring doctor gave the go-ahead to continue — and did so again in the next round. Vince knew he had to act and came in with a flurry of rights that had me reeling. My legs wouldn't obey me as I staggered backwards. It was then that the referee called an end to the battle.

101

We both ended up in hospital. Vince was never the same fighter again, losing his title less than two years later. I was mentally shattered and it took a lot of soul-searching before I was ready to start the long haul back to the top again.

A lot of people in the media and elsewhere wanted me to retire after the defeat by Phillips. But I wasn't going to listen to anyone except myself. I mulled it over and eventually decided on what I thought was right for me. I returned to the ring to try again. As history showed, it *was* the right decision.

I made my mind up that I needed to prepare for future fights in a training camp — and I chose the Australian Institute of Sport in Canberra, base for four or five world champions in other sports. It proved to be the ideal location to begin each of my campaigns. For my first 'comeback' fight I chose Ismael Chaves of Argentina, ranked Number 3 contender for the WBC title and unbeaten in the previous five years. The bout was

'Kostya proved what a real champion he was after the defeat by Vince Phillips. He looked for answers not excuses. And when he found those answers he went away and got on with the job of rebuilding his career. That he did so — and did so with such success — is a measure of Kostya's greatness.'

triple world champion Jeff Fenech

A torrid clash between two gladiators

scheduled for Stocklands Stadium (now Dairy Farmers Stadium) in Townsville, the home of the North Queensland Cowboys rugby league team. As one of my sparring partners I used Jake Rodriguez, the man I had beaten to win the IBF crown. He helped tune me up perfectly. And Chaves never knew what hit him. I don't know how he even made it through to the third round, where I finally destroyed him.

The Chaves fight was supposed to have been a world title eliminator. But who can ever understand boxing politics? I had to keep fighting — and fighting big names — if I was to get another world championship bout. My next opponent, American Calvin Grove, was such a name. He was well known to Australian fans having beaten two of our former world champions, Jeff Fenech and Lester Ellis. And I wasn't taking him lightly. I even managed to shut out from my mind the news that I had lost my court case, a decision handed down in the lead-up to the fight. Grove was shocked by the ferocity of my attack. I knocked him down in the first five seconds of the first round. I chased him around the ring. Down he went again. He struggled to his feet but I pinned him against the ropes. The referee finally stepped in to halt the punishment as the round drew to a close.

Three months later it was an official WBC eliminator against Mexican Rafael Ruelas, a former IBF world lightweight champ. This was a case of into the lion's den as the bout was staged at El Paso which, with its twin city across the Rio Grande River, Ciudad Juarez, sits astride the US-Mexican border. But the screaming crowd did not worry me. I caught him with a powerhouse right in Round One and from then he went on the back foot trying to stay away from me. I hit him with every punch in my repertoire but couldn't put him away. In the ninth round the referee eventually showed some mercy and stopped the fight.

I was now ready to win a world title again. I was due to take on another Mexican, Miguel Angel Gonzalez, at Indio in California, for the vacant WBC super-lightweight title. But a couple of days before I was due to leave Australia he pulled out injured and Cuban exile Diobelys Hurtado stepped into the breach. The WBC demanded that the winner immediately defend the title against Gonzalez. I was lucky that one of my two sparring partners had fought Hurtado and could give me some pointers as to his strengths and weaknesses. I knocked Hurtado down in the first round, but then caught a glancing blow myself with the result that a big swelling began under my right eye. We went punch for

The end for Hurtado came in Round Five — and I again had a world championship belt

punch until I caught him with a real cruncher in the fifth round. He fell like a deflated balloon. Although he managed to regain his feet he staggered like a drunken sailor and the referee, James Jenkin, stepped in and called off the fight.

I was WBC world champion. Now I would continue my quest to become the first boxer in history to unify all three major titles in my division.

The mandatory encounter with Miguel Angel Gonzalez, a former WBC world lightweight champion, was postponed a couple of times, stretching the time I had been out of action to nine months. Looking back, this period of inaction was really nothing, but at the time critics would use it as an excuse to question my ability to beat the Mexican. They seemed to ignore the fact that Gonzalez had been out of the ring even longer — 13 months. But eventually the fight was on, in Miami, Florida, in August 1999. Gonzalez, who had never been knocked out in any of his previous 45 bouts, had been cocky before the fight, but once in the ring I knew I had his measure. Only his pride kept him from going down under the mass of blows I landed on him. At one stage the referee, Frank Santore Jnr, halted proceedings and went to his corner to ask whether his trainer, Abel Sanchez, wanted to throw in the towel. The trainer shook his head. But two rounds later Sanchez had second thoughts and jumped up onto the apron of the ring and conceded defeat. How I wished he had agreed the first time and saved Gonzalez from all that extra punishment.

Making a trunk call. After my defeat of Gonzales, I took time out to take the family on a holiday to Thailand. Everyone knows how I love animals and have a menagerie at home. But I don't think the neighbours in Carss Park would appreciate me having a pet of this size!

Miguel Angel Gonzalez bravely took all the punishment I dished out until his corner threw in the towel in the 10th round

Mexican Ahmed Santos was my next opponent. The bout was at Uncasville, a nondescript town north-west of New York. I had little trouble with him and after I knocked him down twice in the eighth round, the referee halted the bout. Fighting on the undercard that same night was a loudmouth American, Zab Judah, who beat a former victim of mine, Jan Piet Bergman for the vacant IBF world title. Judah jumped into the ring after my victory to try to steal some of the limelight. I suggested he should show more respect. Later he told some American journalists: 'I respect him, but nothing like the way he's going to respect me when I beat him. He's not a champ, he's a chump.' Never mind, I would have the last laugh.

'I would continue my quest to become the first boxer in history to unify all three major titles in my division'

Kostya

Here I am shaping up before the fight against the legendary Julio Cesar Chavez. The Mexican faithful called him Angelito, the Angel of Destruction. Until we met in Phoenix, Arizona, in July 2000 he had lost only four of 109 bouts he had fought over a period of 20 years in the professional ring. He had held world titles in three different weight divisions and fought for a world crown in a fourth. Only one man had knocked him off his feet — another boxing great, Oscar De la Hoya. I was to become the second

DOUBLE CELEBRATION

What a great year — world champion again and a new son. Nikita's baptism was on 24 December 1998. His godparents were my sister Olga and my good mate Olympian Alex Popov. Babushka (grandma) is cuddling baby Nikita, the star of the Russian Orthodox service.

I move in for the kill in the sixth round

DESTROYING THE ANGEL OF DESTRUCTION

I FOUGHT JULIO CESAR CHAVEZ in front of 18,000 xenophobic Mexicans who had poured across the border to watch the encounter. I found out later they were shouting 'Matale', Spanish for 'Kill him', as I made my way to the ring. So you can imagine how horrified they were when in the sixth round I put Chavez down on the canvas with a perfectly timed right to the chin. He tried to shake the cobwebs from his head, but it was to no avail as I went in for the kill. Bang, bang, bang! My punches rained on him and the referee thankfully stopped the bout just as Chavez's crew threw in the towel to save him from further punishment. The crowd went berserk and we had a hairy trip back to the dressing room avoiding all sorts of missiles that were thrown at us. Even plastic chairs came whistling through the air. But Chavez was gracious in defeat, saying: 'I gave my best, but my body did not respond. I am very sad. Forgive me. I apologise to the Latin people.'

The next step in my quest to unify the titles came at Las Vegas in February 2001. My opponent was another American who liked to talk big, the holder of the WBA version of the world title, Sharmba Mitchell. He always referred to himself as 'a warrior' cashing in on the fact he had been named after the king of some African tribe. He also used to fight wearing an imitation African warrior 'skirt' instead of normal boxing trunks. He was full of bravado. 'I rate myself among the best boxers of all time,' he boasted.

JAY LARKIN

The New York-based senior vice-president and executive producer of boxing and other sports for the American PayTV corporation Showtime. Most of Kostya's fights in the new millennium were televised by Showtime.

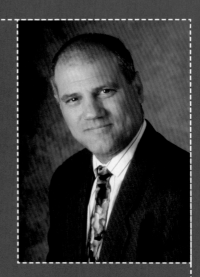

WHAT YOU SEE IS WHAT YOU GET

There is something very special about Kostya. It's hard to put into words, but I saw it for the first time when I watched him as an amateur. He stood out from the rest, most of whom, quite frankly, looked just that … amateur. I saw it again when watching his first professional bout, on the undercard to the Jeff Fenech-Azumah Nelson world title bout in Melbourne in 1992.

There he was, with this mohawk-style haircut, totally fixed on the task ahead. He had a charisma you seldom see in a boxer. There are hundreds of good boxers in the world at any one time. But there are not many with charisma. There are plenty of cocky fighters … arrogant loudmouths. They tend to use their outrageous personalities as a shield, as a facade.

With Kostya, what you see is what you get. He is the ultimate workman, a professional assassin in the ring — quiet, cold and calculating. And once he has demolished his opponent, there is no fuss. He quietly packs up his kit and goes home. There's none of the nonsense of other boxers: no histrionics, no huge entourage trying to get the television cameras' attention. There is just him and his father Boris hugging each other with unashamed affection. Actually, it's quite refreshing.

He reminds me a bit of one of my favourite old-time fighters, 'Marvelous' Marvin Hagler. He, too, would go about his business with a minimum of fuss.

As someone trying to sell Kostya to the sports fans of America I would like him to be a bit more outspoken … a bit more larger than life. In the US we have to compete for the headlines with footballers, baseball stars and basketball celebrities. They get headlines when they play well and bigger headlines when they misbehave … you know … women and steroids. We, in the sport of boxing, get relatively minimal space.

But Kostya's elegance and dignity is good for boxing. He is the ultimate of what a fighter should be. Australians should be proud of this wonderful ambassador.

Australians should be proud of this wonderful ambassador.

Jay Larkin

On the day of the weigh-in, WBC president Jose Sulaiman revealed I had been named one of the 10 best boxers of the 1990s. That was a real pat on the back. Mitchell was obviously worried and started making excuses in the hours before the fight. First he said he was ill. Then he claimed a chronic knee injury might hamper him during the fight. I knew then that I had won the bout psychologically before we had even traded blows. He spent most of each round trying to clinch, but I still managed to get him with a lot of solid blows, one punch opening a horrific gash over his right eye and another splitting his bottom lip. I kept putting him on the canvas. In the seventh round he was down for the fifth time and his team threw in the towel, claiming he had twisted a leg and could not stand unaided. It was an excuse that was to later get him a rematch with me.

I now had two of the major world titles. It was time to go after Judah to get the third. Zab was quick to start mouthing off, claiming he would punch holes in me like a piece of Swiss cheese. Good luck!

A perfect straight left to Mitchell's jaw

SILENCING A LOUDMOUTH

IN PREPARATION FOR THE ENCOUNTER with Judah, in June 2001 I made a mandatory defence of my WBC title at Uncasville against Istanbul-born Oktay Urkal. It was strange evening. One of the early fights involved Vince Phillips, who had taken the IBF title from me. And in the major preliminary bout Judah himself was fighting, successfully defending his crown with a third-round knockout of Allan Vester from Denmark. Judah then sat ringside to watch me in action and spent the whole of my fight shouting out insults. I didn't hear any of them — when I fight I am focused entirely on my opponent and block out all external distractions. Urkal provided an ideal preparation for the Judah clash. The German took me the full 12 rounds. It was a brave effort as it later transpired one of my punches in the seventh round had broken his jaw.

The day of reckoning was set for 2 November 2001. The venue was the MGM Grand Casino in Las Vegas where I had won my first world title. I would put my WBC and WBA crowns on the line, and Judah his IBF title. The lead-up to the unification bout was characterised by a succession of boasts by Judah and efforts to belittle me at every opportunity. But his attempts to play mind games were ham-fisted. I floored him with some simple psychology. I knew that a couple of months earlier he had become the father of a baby girl named Destiny. At the weigh-in 24 hours before our fight he stepped towards me in an aggressive manner. I just smiled, threw an arm around him and asked: 'How's your daughter getting on?' He was taken aback and could only mumble: 'Ah, um, okay.'

115

'Having children is a great experience, isn't it? Better even than winning a world title?'

I then whispered in his ear: 'Having children is a great experience, isn't it? Better even than winning a world title?' He didn't know what to say. I had won the psychological battle. Next it would be the physical war.

In the first round of our fight, he gave me a torrid time and had the one-eyed American media predicting my early demise. But most of his flashy jabs were missing or not hurting me one bit. Then everything changed. In Round Two I began to steer him around the ring, even though he was unaware of what I was doing. Near the end of the round I feinted and he took the bait. I hit him in the neck with a left jab and as he rolled with the punch I whacked a vicious right into his head. Then another solid right. He went spinning to the ground. His head hit the canvas with an almighty thud. Judah got to his feet but his legs refused to do what he wanted. Some journalists described his efforts as looking like an out-of-control rap dancer. Others suggested his legs had turned into spaghetti. It was like a drunk at hotel closing time. As referee Jay Nady gestured that the bout was over, Judah fell flat on his face. Almost every boxing fan who has spoken to me since has a vivid recollection of Judah's final moments in that fight.

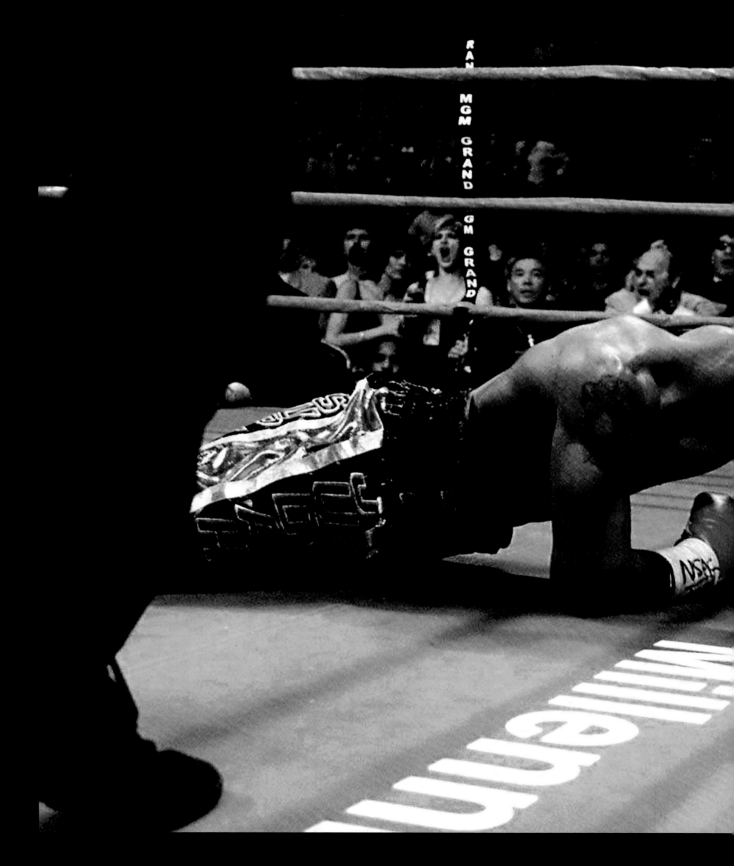

Zab had boasted before the fight: 'Winner takes all!' And I was the winner. When his head began to clear and he realised what had happened, Judah went ballistic. Screaming with disbelief, he zeroed in on the referee and pushed a fist into his throat. Security men were needed to pull him off Nady.

In hindsight, I think this victory was the finest moment in my boxing career. I called it 'my destiny'.

Six months later I returned to the city of my greatest triumph, Las Vegas — but at a different venue, the Mandalay Bay Casino. I was matched with Ben 'Wonder' Tackie from Ghana. He was a tough competitor, refusing to give up even though I continually rained blows on him for the entire 12 rounds. To use that wonderful Aussie expression, I hit him with everything but the kitchen sink. It was left to the judges to give me victory by a substantial number of points.

I catch Ben Tackie with a solid left to the head

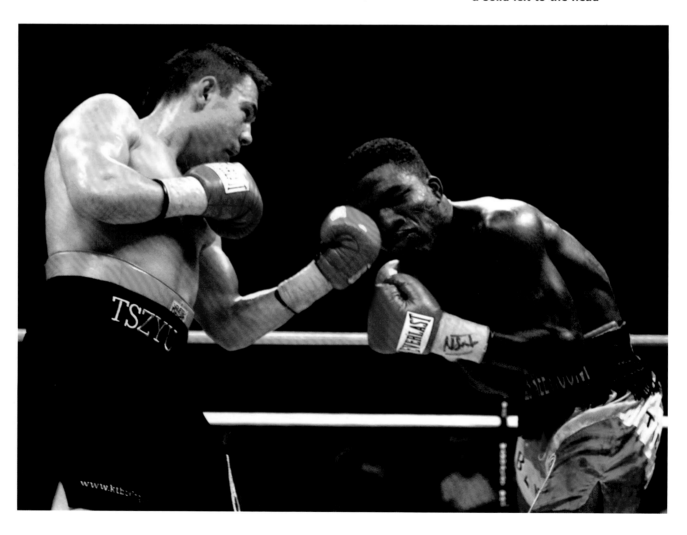

Leija took every punch I threw at him, but refused to surrender

For my next defence of the titles trifecta, I decided to come home. It would be my first fight in Australia in just under five years. Local promoters find it hard to match the money offered in the United States, especially from the big casinos who want major events to attract punters who will spend money in their gambling palaces. But I felt I owed it to my Australian fans to have a 'hometown' bout.

The fight against Texan 'Jesse' James Leija was staged at the Telstra Dome in Melbourne on a Sunday afternoon so it could be beamed back to the United States for primetime television on Saturday night. He was different to most of the big-name American boxers in so far as he wasn't a braggart. Jesse James was like me. He respected his opponents and never badmouthed anyone. Yet he was dangerous in the ring.

In the first couple of rounds my timing was astray, but eventually I found a rhythm and began to blast him with some of my heavy artillery. At the end of the sixth round it was over. Apparently one of my punches had burst his right eardrum and he was in unbearable pain. I described him at the time as 'a true warrior'.

I have been plagued by pre-fight injuries almost as long as I can remember. But like the severed finger tendons before the 1988 Seoul Olympics and the three different injuries I had before the fight against Pedro Sanchez, they never stopped me from making it into the ring.

In 2003 all that changed when I was hit with a double whammy. I was scheduled to defend my crowns against an old opponent, Sharmba Mitchell. It was never my policy to have rematches as I felt to take on a fighter I had already beaten was a backward step. But the IBF had Mitchell as the Number 1 contender and it was a mandatory defence. The fight was scheduled for September in the Russian capital of Moscow.

Entrepreneur Glenn Wheatley was involved in the staging of my bout with Jesse James Leija. Here he is after the fight with me and promoter Vlad Warton

Tim and Jimmy Gestakovski were delighted with my win over Leija

Who says I have any problems in losing weight?

I was looking forward to fighting in the land of my birth for the first time as a professional. However, three months before the fight, after a game of indoor soccer in the gym, my left ankle gave way. I had snapped my Achilles tendon. The fight was off — postponed until February.

I recovered quicker than the doctors thought humanly possible and then came the second blow. Four days before I was due to fly out of Sydney for the fight, I badly tore a muscle in my left shoulder. It meant I could not throw a punch with my left arm. The bout was off again.

By the time I was ready to fight, the WBC and the WBA had decided someone else should be champion, even though I still held the universally accepted world title belt sanctioned by *The Ring* magazine, the bible of boxing, and had not been beaten in the ring.

Most of the American critics had written me off by the time I shaped up against Mitchell at the Glendale Arena in Phoenix, Arizona, where four years earlier I had that stirring victory over Julio Cesar Chavez. They reckoned I would be too rusty after 22 months without a fight. Did I have a surprise for the unbelievers!

Once again I went into the fight with a major injury. But I kept it secret from everyone. Even my sparring partners didn't know I had damaged muscles in the area around my ribs and needed painkilling injections. The fight proved much easier than our first encounter. In the second round I put Sharmba on the canvas with a series of hard rights. Although he lasted through the round, the end was inevitable. I went after him and after I knocked him down another three times, referee Raul Caiz stepped in and mercifully stopped the fight.

I had proved the critics wrong. Johnny Lewis said he doubted whether I had ever fought a better fight.

123

After two sons, our first daughter, Anastasia, was born on 21 September 2002. I wasn't kidding when I told Zab Judah that the birth of one's child was better than winning a world title. And I have been so blessed three times. I can hardly put my feelings into words, but when I held each of them in my arms for the first time I was truly overwhelmed.

ERIC RASKIN

Award-winning American boxing writer. He was managing editor of The Ring *magazine, regarded as the sport's bible, for almost eight years until going freelance in 2005. Raskin still writes for The Ring as well as the influential website Maxboxing.com.*

A TRUE CHAMPION

Kostya Tszyu is clearly one of the greatest junior welterweights of all time, thanks in large part to the fact that he has never strayed from this weight division. Legendary Mexican Julio Cesar Chavez certainly had a more exceptional run at the weight, but aside from him, Tszyu has the most impressive resume in terms of what he's done at 140 pounds.

As for the past decade, Tszyu stands out from other boxers for several reasons. First there is his longevity. How many fighters go eight straight years without a loss against consistently first-rate competition? He possesses arguably the greatest straight right hand of his generation. And then there is the fact that he unified all the so-called alphabet titles (WBC, WBA and IBF) in his division. Only a handful of his contemporaries have managed that feat. *The Ring* magazine awarded him its world championship belt because that is what he was — a world champion, not like some of the alphabet titleholders. Since the 1920s, *The Ring* had told people who the champions were, and in 2001 Editor-in-Chief Nigel Collins recognised that the time was right for the magazine to clarify matters all over again. Bernard Hopkins had just unified the middleweight crown and Tszyu had done the same in the junior-welterweight division. Before the myriad of governing bodies could find lame excuses to strip the champs of their hard-won glory, we declared them holders of a title they could only lose the old-fashioned way — inside the ropes.

The disgraceful manner in which Kostya was stripped of two of his belts (WBC and WBA) perfectly underscores why the public and the media need to ignore the alphabet bandits and recognise *The Ring* titles. Kostya became the division's only champion when he kayoed Zab Judah. And he would remain the division's only champion until he either left the division or someone beat him in the ring. It is simple logic, really. But the alphabets refuse to be logical. Yet I'm glad Kostya let himself be stripped rather than make pointless mandatory defences. Anyway, he knows the importance of *The Ring* belt.

His performance against Sharmba Mitchell definitely surprised me. Like the majority of American writers, I picked the more active Mitchell to win, and I couldn't have been more wrong. Tszyu destroyed Sharmba. I think it was the most perfect performance of his career.

When his career is finally over, history will remember him as a great puncher and a dominant champion. But sadly he will also be remembered as a fighter who never became a huge star in America despite having the talent and exciting style to achieve great popularity. I think his lack of activity — fighting just once or twice a year — was largely to blame. But that probably helped him to stay longer in the sport.

The Tszyus all love the sauna. Here
I am in 1999 with Papa, Tim (5)
and Nikita (seven months)

Papa shows the best way to follow up a sauna — jump straight into
the (Russian) snow. Unfortunately Sydney's sun does not allow for that
possibility. But a dip in a cool pool is the next best thing

My sister Olga and her husband Igor with their two children, Daniel and Denis

Nikita and Tim enjoying the backyard pool

I love my beautiful girl

Papa has slotted into Aussie life so well. Here he shows Timophey how to drive the barbie while Nikita guards the salad

Growing fast. Timophey, Nikita and Anastasia in October 2002

Real men love their footy. Three Tszyu generations cheering on their favourite rugby league team, the St George Illawarra Dragons

My brother-in-law Igor Goloubev teaching Nikita and a mate the finer points of the sport at the Tszyu Boxing Academy

However much I love Australia I never tire of going back to Serov. Every time I am there, I get together with mates from the past. Here I am with some friends from my schooldays and boxers who were with me at Chernya's

Starting young. Tim is just
18 months old but already
wants to be like his father

SWEET AS SUGAR

PEOPLE OFTEN ASK ME how I would shape up to some of the great boxers of the past. Of course, it's all hypothetical. Many of the legends of boxing were in weight divisions far removed from mine. After all, you could never imagine me in the same ring as the great Muhammad Ali or that other magnificent heavyweight Rocky Marciano.

But if I had a time machine, I would like to go back 60 years and take on that great crowd-pleaser Sugar Ray Robinson who, when he won his first world title, was a welterweight, the division above mine.

His name says it all. When he started his career in 1940 someone commented to his trainer that Robinson was 'a sweet fighter', to which the trainer replied: 'Yes, he's as sweet as sugar!'

I think Sugar Ray Robinson versus Kostya Tszyu would be a very interesting fight.

Like me, Robinson had a great amateur career. I'm told he won 40 of his 85 bouts with first-round knockouts. As a professional he lost only 19 of an incredible 202 bouts over 25 years. He held the world welterweight title for four years. He relinquished it unbeaten and moved up to middleweight where he won eight world title bouts in a period of seven years. And he even had a shot at the world light-heavyweight crown.

The guy was great. One of the greatest fighters ever. Most boxers of his era never knew how to fight him. I've watched films of some of his fights and realised just how devastating he was. He had unbelievable punching power. His punches would come from every conceivable angle. And he had great determination.

Sugar Ray Robinson in one of his most famous fights — beating Jake LaMotta, the so-called Bronx Bull, to win the world middleweight title, at Chicago in 1951. It was sweet revenge for Sugar Ray. Eight years earlier LaMotta had been the first boxer to beat Robinson after an unbeaten run in his first 40 professional bouts. After that setback Sugar Ray had another 89 straight bouts before his next defeat

If I had been matched with him I really would have had to do my homework. I would have had to study everything he did in the ring. He did get beaten when he was at his top, so there must have been a flaw or two … some chink in his armour … although they weren't obvious.

Out of the ring he had such a positive personality and a wonderful trademark smile. He had the right image for our sport.

And who would win in a match-up between Sugar Ray and Kostya? I'll leave it to the experts to decide that!

'If I had been matched with [Sugar Ray] I really would have had to do my homework'

Kostya

Out of the ring he had such a positive personality and a wonderful trademark smile

THE CELEBRITY-GO-ROUND

ONE OF THE PERKS OF BEING A WORLD CHAMPION is that you get to meet some famous people. As a kid growing up in Serov I would never have imagined chatting on first-name terms with world political leaders, explorers of outer space, Olympic champions, Hollywood legends and pop stars. But my world title belts certainly provided an introduction to the headline makers of the 20th and 21st centuries.

139

Who would have thought Nicole Kidman was a fight fan?

I have some great friends among the elite Russian sportsmen. Here is a couple I caught up with at the 1996 Atlanta Olympics. There is no need to explain the record of swimmer Alexander Popov. He is one of the greatest in the history of his sport. He won gold medals in the freestyle sprint double (50m and 100m) at both the 1992 Barcelona and 1996 Atlanta Olympics, but lost his titles at Sydney four years later when he took out silver 100m.

He retired after missing out on the medals at the 2004 Athens Olympics. But, together with the relays he finished with a total of four Olympic gold and six silver. At world championships he won five gold medals. I knew Alex through our time training at the Australian Institute of Sport in Canberra, where his long-time coach Gennadi Touretski was based. Alex became a very close friend and is godfather to Nikita.

My other mate pictured here is a Russian hero, Aleksandr Karelin, although few people in Australia would know about his incredible record in Greco-Roman wrestling. In Atlanta, just three months after undergoing a major shoulder operation, he became the first wrestler to win a gold medal in the same weight division — in his case the super-heavyweight — three times, adding to his Seoul and Barcelona successes. At that stage he had been unbeaten for nine years. In 1999 he won his 12th world or Olympic gold medal.

At the world titles a year before Atlanta one of his ribs was broken in an early match — but he went on to win gold. 'I didn't want to appear weak and skip a bout because of something as trifling as a broken rib,' he explained. Tough? You had better believe it.

141

Larisa Dolina is arguably Russia's greatest female pop star — although she is best known for her jazz. I met up with her and we became friends during her Australian tour in 2001. And she even came to the gym for a spar. Later Larisa agreed to record my anthem 'Something Worth Fighting For'. And it was to this song that I made my way to the ring for the Zab Judah fight

It's great catching up with fellow Russian sports stars when I make my regular trips back to Moscow. One of the greatest was legendary ice hockey player Vyatchslav (Slava) Fetisov. An incredibly fast and strong defenceman, he was the backbone of Soviet sides during the 1980s. Sides in which Slava starred won two Olympic gold medals (at Sarejevo in 1984 and Calgary in 1988) and a bronze (at Lake Placid, 1980). When he retired in 2000, at the age of 41, he had one last testimonial match in Moscow, playing for the Russian All-Stars. But he donated all the money to the families of the 188 crew who lost their lives when the nuclear submarine *Kursk* sank after an on-board explosion in the Barents Sea a few days earlier. Slava is now Russia's Minister for Sport

The right shoulder's hurting a bit after a tough fight. But I am pleased to have friends around like the two Russian-born pole vaulters who competed for Australia in the 2000 Sydney Olympics. Tatania Grigorieva won a silver medal, her husband Viktor Christiakov finished equal fifth. With us is Sergeant Jim Duignan who runs the Rockdale Police Citizens Youth Club (PCYC) where the Tszyu Boxing Academy is located

I am welcomed back to Russia in 2001 by Eduard Rossel, the charismatic Governor of the Sverdlovsky region in the Urals in which Serov is located. Rossel, the first governor in modern Russian history, is a pioneer in Russia's current policy of federalism

Two famous sons of Serov. Back in my home town I take time to meet the Mayor of Serov, Vladimir Anisimov

Russian presidents? It doesn't happen every day, but I have caught up with Boris Yeltsin (seen here with Natasha and me) and his successor Vladimir Putin (right). I met Putin in late 2004 when I was invited to his dacha (villa) at Novo-Ogaryovo on the outskirts of Moscow during a trip to my homeland to receive an award as the Russian Sports Star of the Year (for atheletes living abroad)

On one visit to Moscow I caught up with one of the pioneers of space, cosmonaut Pavel Popovich (left). He was the fourth Russian in space, being rocketed aloft in 1962, a year after the first spaceman, fellow Russian Yuri Gagarin, made a circuit of the earth. As commander of Vostok 4, Popovitch spent almost three days in space. He was to go up a second time 12 years later as commander of Soyuz 14. During 16 days in space, his craft docked with the Salut 3 space station. What incredible courage Pavel and his fellow space travellers showed!

The best in the world. Some high jinks before the celebrity race at the 2005 Australian Formula One Grand Prix in Melbourne. Lauren Burns, taekwondo gold medal winner at the 2000 Sydney Olympics, has an unfair advantage over me as she can use her feet in her sporting discipline

Formula for success. A journalist from the BBC once said Vlado's Charcoal Grill in the Melbourne suburb of Richmond was the best steak restaurant in the world. I'm not going to disagree. Croation Vlado Gregurek came to Australia as a young man and 33 years ago opened his first steakhouse. These days it's a regular haunt for celebrities. And that's where I caught up with German motor racing star Michael Schumacher during Grand Prix Week in Melbourne

World 400m hurdles champion Jana Pittman was a picture of courage as she strived to overcome injury the 2004 Athens Olympics. I knew exactly how she had felt, after a battle to overcome Achilles heel an shoulder injuries before successfully defending my world crown against Sharmba Mitchell the same ye

Another Aussie star. Television host Rove McManus, a Gold Logie winner

More Australians phenomena successful on the world stage The Wiggles (left) and Hi 5 (above) are celebrities even n kids are excited about meetin

Anyone for tennis? (Left to right) Team Tszyu's security chief Glen Jennings, Mark 'The Scud' Philippoussis, me and Johnny Lewis during a break in training in Melbourne

I've learned to love rugby league since moving to Australia. Sadly Max Krilich was captain of Australia before my arrival so I never saw him play

Mr Soccer. Les Murray is a great European who made it in his adoptive country of Australia

Here I am at Rosehill races in Sydney. I mark down in my racebook the tips given to me by famous racecaller Des Hoysted

I shape up with some of Sydney's finest jockeys

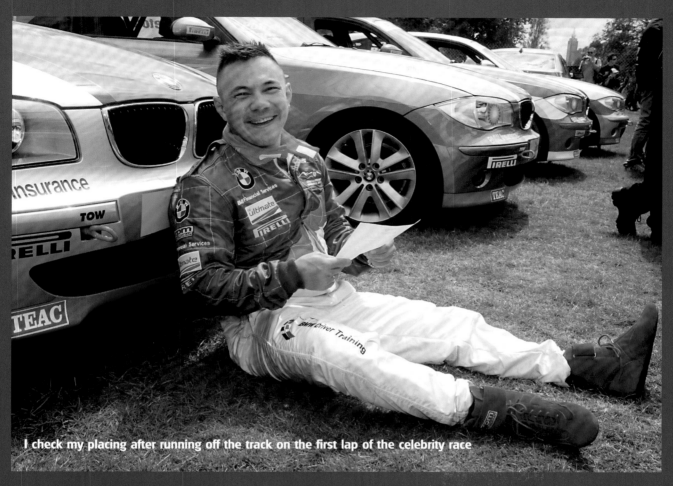

I check my placing after running off the track on the first lap of the celebrity race

One of my best mates, Alexander Lebzyak. Our friendship goes back to even before we were teammates at the 1990 Goodwill Games. He won the gold medal in the light-heavy-weight division at the 1997 World Championships in Hungary and at the 2000 Sydney Olympics. Today he is head coach of the Russian amateur boxing team

LORDS OF THE RING

I ONCE READ A QUOTE FROM HARRY BATH, a famous old player from the St George Dragons (the club I follow in the National Rugby League competition). He said: 'Those who drink at the well should never forget those who dug the well.' In other words, remember and cherish the deeds of the sportsmen and women who came before you. I certainly do. And that's why I take every opportunity to mix with boxers past and present.

I've run up against the likes of Vic Patrick, one of Australia's greatest fighters. His real name was Victor Patrick Lucca and he was born in the tough Sydney suburb of Woolloomooloo in 1920. Fighting in the late 1940s and early 1950s, Vic never got the chance to fight for a world title — but he thoroughly deserved to have done so. He won 50 fights, lost four and drew one, fighting many of the best of his era. He was later a publican in Woolloomooloo and a respected boxing referee.

At some of the boxing reunions I've also caught up with another immigrant like myself, Rocky Gattellari. He holds a special record — when he was beaten in a world flyweight title bout by Italian Salvatore Burruni at the Sydney Showground in December 1965 it was the first WBC world championship bout ever staged. Until then, there had been only one undisputed world champion in each division instead of the many so-called alphabet crowns now in existence.

151

What a line-up of champs! Here I am with (left to right)
Jeff Fenech, Vic Patrick, Danny Green and Rocky Gattellari

In recent years I've also spent time with some of the current stars of my sport. In 2002 I trained with the great American boxer Roy Jones Junior. Talk about alphabet soup — at that time he held no less than seven world or American titles from different boxing organisations — the WBC, WBA, IBF, IBO, WBF, IBA and NBA. The mind boggles! We had both fought at the 1988 Seoul Olympics where Roy had been robbed of a gold medal in the light-middleweight division by an outrageous decision by the judges.

I regularly catch up with some of Australia's other boxers who have made their mark on the world scene including Danny Green (WBC interim super-middleweight champ), Sam 'King' Soliman (won IBF middleweight eliminator), Vic Darchinyan (IBF and IBO world flyweight titles) and former Dragons rugby league star Anthony Mundine (WBA super-middleweight champion).

Like me, Rocky Gattellari was an Olympian who made a name for himself in his adopted country

Vic Patrick offers me advice gleaned from his years in the ring

Jeff Fenech

Boxing great Roy Jones Jnr with me, Papa, Tim and my nephew Daniel

Who's 'The Man'? With Anthony Mundine

153

My old friend, great American boxer
Roy Jones Junior and I after training
together at my gym in Rockdale in 2002

Another Aussie world champ, Danny Green

… and who's 'The King'? Thumbs up for Sam Soliman

With Vic Darchinyan

RUSSELL CROWE

Hollywood actor Russell Crowe, who won an Oscar in 2001 for his role in Gladiator, *became a friend while he was filming the movie* Cinderella Man, *about heavyweight boxing champion James J Braddock.*

100 PERCENT A CHAMPION

Kostya Tszyu is a truly great athlete … a sublime athlete who has been the mark in the sand for physical fitness. The first time I saw him in training was an eye-opener. The first thing he did was a 26-minute set of skipping without stopping. Try it one day. It's pretty tough. I'll never forget the focus and the absolute commitment Kostya illustrated to me that day and many times since. He was a dynamo. And when I first attempted his training regimen Kostya was brutally honest. He said: 'Russell, you're not mentally tough enough.'

So I immediately knew I still had plenty of work to do.

Seeing how Kostya got through the shoulder surgery [suffered while preparing for the second Sharmba Mitchell fight] was an inspiration to me when a similar injury took place in the course of my training for *Cinderella Man*. But I am an older man these days and have been carrying injuries since 185AD [a reference to the hit movie *Gladiator*].

Kostya's example has been a source of strength. The great American boxing trainer Angelo Dundee has said Kostya is the best pound-for-pound boxer he has ever seen. Angelo has seen some great fighters in his time, so that's certainly saying something. Kostya is a sublime athlete. He is 100 percent man, 100 percent per cent honourable, and 100 percent a champion.

And his standing in my eyes was not diminished at all by his defeat at the hands of Ricky Hatton in a great fight between two great champions. The fight had everything that a world championship should have. It was Ricky Hatton's night, but this loss in no way lessened Kostya Tszyu's place in the history of boxing. Kostya's graciousness in losing will be remembered by all. He is 100 percent class and 100 percent heart … a true champion and a great Australian.

Winning or losing, it has been a privilege to call Kostya a friend.

A winning combination — Team Tszyu. (From left to right) back row, Peter
Mitrevski, Glen Jennings, Johnny Lewis, me, Dr Bill Anseline, Papa; front row,
Matt Watt, Roman Lyubovny, Igor Goloubev, Paul Upham

A WINNING TEAM

A BOXER MAY BE ALONE IN THE RING for the three minutes of each round. But what happens there depends so much on the team that is behind him — the trainer and seconds in his corner and the backup squad that has helped him in his preparation. I have been blessed with a superb group of hard-working and loyal colleagues. I have spoken elsewhere about my relationship with trainer Johnny Lewis, the man who guided me through my entire professional career. But he is just one member of Team Tszyu.

159

'I have been blessed with a superb group of hard-working and loyal colleagues'

Kostya

GLEN JENNINGS

Security expert who has protected international pop stars such as the Rolling Stones, U2, Michael Jackson, and Madonna when touring Australia. Security director for both the Olympics at Atlanta (1996) and Sydney (2000). He linked with me when I first fought at the Newcastle Entertainment Centre in 1993. Glen currently handles all security, travel and accommodation arrangements for Team Tszyu.

MUTUAL RESPECT

Kostya Tszyu and I go back almost 12 years. Yet it seems like only yesterday that I brought him to Newcastle for a media conference before his fight with Larry LaCoursiere, his eighth professional bout. At the time he could hardly speak a word of English. Basically we communicated with just a nod, a wink and a shrug of the shoulders. We had a bit of a laugh at how hard it was for him to answer questions from the journalists. It was, in fact, a great start, because it meant we both got to know each other without expressing anything in words. And to this day, at any one time, I know pretty much what he is thinking and what he wants and act accordingly.

After that first encounter, each time we met we got on like a house on fire. As time went by we became the firmest of friends. I can honestly say Kostya and I have never had an argument or fight — which says a lot for our friendship because we have been in some very stressful campaigns, where our personalities could easily have boiled over. I believe it is because Kostya and I have a very, very deep mutual respect for each other. It is a respect that is rarely expressed in words, but regularly in simple actions.

Kostya understands my role. I am there for all of his campaigns, to take control of the members of his team and to provide the perfect, distraction-free environment for him to prepare for the task of winning the fight. All issues relating to the team and the training camp have to be dealt with professionally, and without fuss, to ensure a seamless day-to-day preparation for Kostya.

Often that is not as easy as it may seem. A classic example is the second Sharmba Mitchell fight, in Phoenix. One of the things Kostya wants during his preparation for a title defence is that two lots of his training gear are laundered every day. It is almost religious. This is a small issue but very important as we try to ensure Kostya is relaxed and focused … in his comfort zone, so to speak. One evening I bundled up the clothes but on the way to the laundry stopped off at a neighbourhood shop to pick up some groceries. I had only left our van for a few minutes — but when I came out it was gone. Towed away by parking police. I was devastated. Not because the van had been towed away — but because the laundry was still to be done. Bugger the impound fee, the cab fares, and the hassle of the tow-away … the most important thing was ensuring Kostya's training gear was laundered and ready for the next day. It took some time to find the yard where the van had been impounded and sort out the paperwork. But some four hours later, I eventually got the laundry done, with Kostya blissfully unaware of the hiccup.

So often, it's those little things that count!

KT is something of an enigma in the United States. The Yanks cannot work him out at all. The Team Tszyu members arrive without any fanfare, train hard without any loud music, say very little, always show respect and treat people politely. Then Kostya beats up their guys, grabs his belts, says very little and we are on the next plane home to our families. The Yanks are left shaking their heads and wondering 'What happened?' time and time again.

The Team Tszyu group is very close. Most of us have been together for a decade or more, we have a proven formula, and we all work towards one goal: to give our champ the best chance of winning. It is as simple as that.

I am proud to be working for Team Tszyu. And I am even more proud of my mate KT — because he is, and always will be, my best friend.

It's all smiles for me and my mate Glen Jennings on his 40th birthday

Matt Watt has been my manager in recent years, with a bold and innovative attitude to my interests in and out of the ring, with some great merchandising arrangements, sponsorships and fight deals. Glen Jennings is an old friend from the days of my early fights in Newcastle. He owns one of the largest security firms in Australia. As well as handling my security, Glen ensures that everything runs smoothly when we are in camp. My brother-in-law Igor Goloubev is the head coach at my gym in Sydney, the Tszyu Boxing Academy, and helps Johnny Lewis in my corner. Roman Lyubovny is my masseur. There is hardly a muscle in my body that, at some stage, has not been manipulated by Roman. Peter Mitrevski has been in my corner for years and has been a great support for Johnny. Dr Bill Anseline, a more recent addition to Team Tszyu, looks after every aspect of my health and wellbeing. My Papa, Boris, helps ensure my discipline never wavers — and when I am in training eats the same food, trains with me and gives up the little luxuries of life that I am forced to reject as I reach peak fitness. Paul Upham is a fine photojournalist who has chronicled much of my career.

‘My Papa, Boris, helps ensure my discipline never wavers — and when I am in training eats the same food, trains with me and gives up the little luxuries of life that I am forced to reject as I reach peak fitness.’

Kostya

MATTHEW WATT

The former investment banker and television executive helped promote my 2003 bout with 'Jesse' James Leija and then became my manager, guiding me into important world title defences and opening up a lucrative new era of business, including licensing, marketing and endorsements outside the ring.

THE PEOPLE'S CHAMP

Many sportsmen and women who become famous tend to forget their roots and the fans that supported them on their journey to the top. Others hold dear the encouragement they received during the formative years of their sporting careers. Kostya Tszyu personifies this latter group.

He strives to ensure a comfortable life for his parents and his wife Natasha, who were the foundations on which his life as a boxer was built. And he certainly has not lost touch with his fans.

One only has to witness any of Kostya's public appearances — like the run through the streets of Sydney in mid-2005, climaxing with him sparring in Martin Place — to understand what he means to the fans and what they mean to him. Whenever he is out and about, his supporters grab every possible vantage point to cheer their hero. And then they line up in their hundreds to ask for his autograph. Kostya regularly stays past the allotted time in the hope that no fan will be disappointed.

It's more than that cheeky smile of his or the unique hairstyle that attracts people from every socio-economic group, from both sexes and from every generation of Australians. It's Kostya's sincerity that shines through. Members of the general public are never fooled by artificial smiles, handshakes and back-slapping. They know that Kostya is the 'genuine article'.

Even when in training for a fight he still finds time for regular live chats with the fans on his website (www.kostyatszyu.com) answering every conceivable question from, What is your favourite beer? (I like all brands of beer) to Have you ever been scared in a fight? (I've never been scared — I am always confident in my ability) and How do you think a younger Kostya, at, say, 21, would have gone against the fighter you are now? (Kostya now would beat Kostya at 21 — I would wear myself down).

Kostya's universal appeal is obvious as fans from all around the world send their best wishes. Tweedie writes: You have quite a lot of fans over here in Ireland, a lot more than you'd realise. You'd be given a royal welcome if you ever decided to visit.' Kostya tells Tweedie he'd love to have a cold Guinness with him. And he's not joking.

The public appearances … the Internet chats … the book and DVD signing sessions … the tours around the country to meet his fans … the visits to sick or disadvan-taged kids … they show that if one was looking for a simple phrase to describe Kostya Tszyu it would be The People's Champ.

Where's Kostya? Yes, I'm in there amongst the fans. You can pick me by my distinctive hairstyle

MY FANS ARE MY FRIENDS

RIGHT BACK TO MY CHILDHOOD DAYS in Serov, the most important people in my life have always been the members of my family. As mentioned previously, these days I am also reliant on my backup team, who are hands-on and with me 24 hours a day, seven days a week in the countdown to each bout.

Then there is another vital group of people without whom I would never have made it to boxing's Mt Everest and would not have been able to scale the mountain a second time after my first defeat. The fans.

Too many sportsmen and women don't want to have anything to do with their fans, despite the fact that these important people pay their hard-earned money at the turnstiles to watch them in action or buy precious memorabilia. Those so-called sport stars are living in a dream world. A Wollongong journalist once expressed surprise that I appeared to enjoy mixing with the fans.

'You are obviously having fun,' he said. And he was right. These are my people. They cheered me on when I was on my way to my first world title. And they stuck by me through thick and thin when I suffered setbacks. Fans? No, they are more than just supporters. They are my friends. Kids in wheelchairs. Proud fathers showing their sons and daughters what one can achieve with determination and a sense of purpose. Elderly ladies who can relate to my mother who nurtured me in my early years. Policemen who wish that kids in their area would focus on success in sport instead of going off the rails. Wives who see both Natasha and me trying to instill the real values of life in our children.

If I can be a good role model to kids — be they in Australia or Russia or anywhere else in the world — it would be worth 100 world championships. That may sound an exaggeration. Yet my Papa never won a world championship and, as far as I am concerned, he is the greatest role model imaginable.

**Organisers of my first Serov fan club
— Alena and Sacha Amminikov**

Aussie, Aussie, Aussie ... Oi, Oi, Oi!

When it comes to hairstyles,
he certainly is a knockout

Pouring a beer for my new-
found mates at 'the local'

I'm never short of devoted supporters wherever I fight in the world — and the Tszyu Crew and I always celebrate victories together

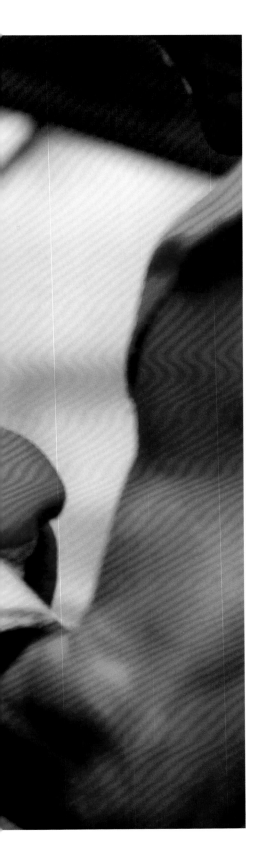

EARLY MORNING SHOCK

MY NEXT TITLE DEFENCE was at the MEN Arena in Manchester, Britain's biggest in-door sporting arena. Some 22,000 supporters of Ricky Hatton turned up at 2am to cheer on their local hero as he challenged for my IBF crown. The fight was scheduled for this ungodly hour so it could be screened at prime time on pay-for-view television in the United States. But at least my fans back home on Australia's east coast could see it at the more sensible time of 11am.

As usual, it was back to the AIS in Canberra for the spartan regimen that I had used in all my previous successful title defences. This time there was even a public exhibition in the centre of Sydney. Police closed off the streets as I ran between Circular Quay and Martin Place where I sparred with Sam 'King' Soliman, number one contender for the IBF world middleweight crown, in front of a lunch-time throng of office workers and tourists. Soliman had given me some torrid sparring sessions before a couple of my other title defences and he had the added bonus of being a heavier man and therefore a heavier puncher than those I would meet in the ring.

171

Sam Soliman gives me a tough workout in front of office workers and shoppers in Sydney's Martin Place

It was a torrid encounter with
Hatton from the opening bell

The British press had given Hatton the nickname 'The Hitman' because of the large number of knockouts on his unbeaten record. But Hitman Hatton was dismissed by many critics because of his reluctance to fight outside his native England, indeed out of his home town of Manchester. Only three times had he fought overseas, the most recent five years before our encounter. He also used to take a lot of heavy punches himself in order to get a knockout. I thought I would be too fast for him.

Someone told me later I should have read the famous piece of poetry by his compatriot Robbie Burns and taken heed: 'The best-laid schemes o' mice and men. Gang aft a-gley, An' lea'e us nought but grief and pain for promis'd joy.' I don't read old English too well — it's hard enough coping with the modern-day language. But basically it says our best-laid plans often go haywire and instead of joy we're left with grief and pain.

So it was in Manchester in the wee hours of 5 June 2005. My world fell down around me. My plans just didn't come off and Ricky took my world title from me. I still don't know how I lost.

Everything had gone according to plan up until the fight. I will eventually work out what went wrong. One day the answer will come to me. But he dug deep and produced a lot more than he had ever produced in any of his 38 earlier fights.

Johnny Lewis had said in Australian newspapers before the fight that Hatton reminded him a lot of his boyhood idol, George Barnes, the British Empire welterweight champion in the 1950s who had worried some world-class fighters. Barnes was fighting a long time before I was born, so I wouldn't know. But Johnny said Barnes, like Hatton, was a short, muscular, working-class hero with relentless style and a willingness to trade punches with anyone. No matter how much punishment George took he was dangerous right until the end of a fight.

That is exactly how Hatton turned out to be. I tried everything to stop him coming forward … everything to put him down. It was a real bar-room brawl. And in the 9th round Ricky hit me with a low blow that had me down on my knees. I still hoped to beat Ricky. But at the end of the 11th round Johnny Lewis took the decision out of my hands. He motioned to the referee that the fight was over. I wanted to continue but Johnny had the final say. He said he was stopping the fight because I was getting hit too much.

I wanted to be among the first to congratulate the new champion. As I explained to the crowd, I had lost to a man who was the better fighter on the night. I told them I had planned lots of things to counter him, but Ricky was better than me in every way.

He in turn was gracious: 'I am sure Kostya would rather go out on his shield like he did tonight. He is a true legend and a great warrior. And I think if he had to lose he would have wanted to lose in a real war like we turned on. You have to have a lot of bottle and courage to fight Kostya Tszyu — to take him head-on and try to get inside his powerful punches. He should have no regrets. If I can achieve half of what Kostya has done in his career, I'll be a very proud man. He's not a champion, but a champion and a half.'

People have come up with all sorts of theories about my loss.

The thousands of fans cheering for Ricky? That wasn't a problem. It was worse with the Mexicans in Phoenix when I fought the legendary Julio Cesar Chavez in 2000. The Manchester fans did not worry me.

The 2am start? There are suggestions that I should have stuck with my original plan to live my life on Australian time and that my decision to change once I reached England backfired. All I can say is that it made no difference.

The battle to shed weight? As usual I had to shed 20kg for the fight. It's always been the case — but perhaps as I get older it may take a bit more of a toll on my body.

The low blow? Some say the referee, Dave Parris, should have penalised Ricky, maybe even disqualified him. Sure it hurt, but I cannot use that as an excuse.

I wonder if the real reason was that my preparation was just too good … maybe too perfect. Nothing went wrong. There were no injuries, no problems. Perhaps because of the near faultless preparation I lost my focus, believing everything was going perfectly to plan. And, of course, everything didn't.

Then there was the fact that Ricky Hatton did more than anyone expected him to do. What can I say? Nothing except 'Good on him'.

That is what sport is all about!

While we were on the plane back to Australia a big story broke. Well, some people might call it a story. It was in fact a disgraceful fabrication. A report from Russia said I had sacked Johnny Lewis because he had

Beaten but unbowed. I'm back among friends in Sydney

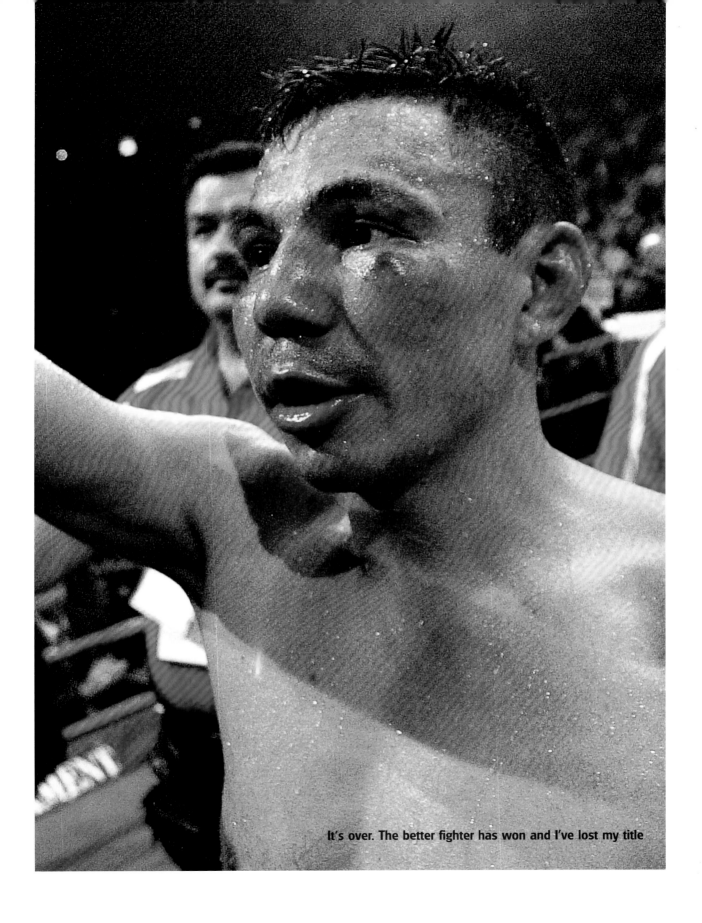

It's over. The better fighter has won and I've lost my title

thrown in the towel. I have since found out where the story began — and I will never trust that person again. The media ran with the story. They wanted sensation. They wanted bulls***. But it never happened.

I wasn't happy when Johnny called off the fight. But I respect his decision. I have to live with it. Johnny and I have been together for a long time and we are still together and will continue to be together. We have been a great team and as a great team we worked hard together over many years. We are still a team. What binds us together is friendship. It's something you cannot buy. You can buy most things but you can't buy trust.

We are still a team

'When Kostya was world champion everyone in Russia respected him. After he was so gallant in defeat, we now all love him.'

renowned Russian singer Iosif Kobzon, in a telephone conversation with Natasha after the Ricky Hatton bout

NATASHA TSZYU

My wife, my lover, my best friend, my children's mother, my confidante, my adviser … the rock on which my life is built. I first knew her as Natasha Anikina, a hairdresser who worked in a salon in Serov. We met in a group of friends around the time I was preparing for the 1988 Seoul Olympics. We were soon inseparable.

MY MAN, MY HERO

Kostya is everything for me. He's my husband, he's my godfather, he's my mum, he's my dad. I reckon he is the best person I could ever have hoped to meet.

I had led a pretty mundane life until I met Kostya. After work I and a few of my friends would go for a drink and we ended up in the same group as Kostya. He was quite famous at that stage. I was very shy and almost scared to even talk to him. He was wonderful. There was no ego and he was so polite to everyone he met, not how I thought a famous sportsman would be. He was what Aussies would call 'true blue'.

Things eventually got serious and somehow I knew that we would one day marry and have children. But never did I envisage our life would be shared in a foreign country we would one day call our own. When he decided to move to Australia it was natural that I would go with him. Times were hard. I missed my family. I missed Russia. And I found it hard learning not only a new language but a new way of life. I cried myself to sleep night after night. I wanted to go home to Serov.

Kostya was homesick too. But he coped so much better than I did because of his incredible self-will, something he has shown in all of his fights. A dogged determination to succeed, no matter what the odds. Together we survived and built the foundations for a long and wonderful life together.

He can be such an uncompromising man in the boxing ring. But I have been privileged to see the other side of Kostya Tszyu. Outside the ring he can be a real softie. Although he likes to hide this side of his character it comes through when he meets underprivileged kids or youngsters with disabilities. They are very special to him.

He was such a help during my pregnancies, especially when I was expecting our first, Timophey (named after Kostya's grandfather) when he worked his training schedules around our parenting classes. And with Anastasia, our latest child, he shocked the doctors by doing push-ups in the delivery ward. He had realised after being there at the birth of Timophey and Nikita just how exhausting the labour had been for me. He told me he was going to share that exhaustion — between every contraction he would do 50 push-ups. That was okay early in the labour when the contractions only came every eight or 10 minutes, but nearer the birth, when they were down to every 40 seconds or so, he was struggling. It wasn't quite what I was experiencing, but I loved him so much for trying to match my fatigue. It will be something we'll be able to tell Anastasia when she is old enough to understand.

Pregnancy? When it comes time to prepare for a fight, I laughingly compare Kostya to a pregnant woman. He's no longer his fun-loving self but gets in funny moods. Although it can be hard on us, the kids and I understand how he feels and try to help by giving him all the support he needs.

I couldn't give him help when he needed it most — in the ring when he first lost his world title, to Vince Phillips in Atlantic City in 1997. I was two months pregnant at the time (with Nikita) and I had trouble sleeping and was plagued with morning sickness every day.

Watching the fight was the worst experience in my life. I had never seen him being beaten, so I had no idea what to do or what to think. At one stage I wanted to jump into the ring and stop the fight — but I knew I never could. I was crying my eyes out by the end of the fight. But I managed to stop crying before I went into the ring to comfort him. I knew that Kostya, in his hour of defeat, needed me to be strong. So I masked my emotions as I cuddled my beaten hero. Back home he went through mental torture and none of the family knew what to say or do to help. Those months after the Phillips loss put an incredible strain on our marriage. But hurdles are put there for a purpose. Once you get over them you are a better person. And we jumped this hurdle.

Kostya eventually began to spark again. The Kostya of old returned as he prepared to climb the mountain once again. And when he managed to win not just one, but all three major world titles, the Phillips fight became just a dim, distant memory.

After the horrible experience of the fight against Phillips I decided never again to watch any of Kostya's fights — either live in the stadium or on television. Early on each day he was be fighting, I would go to the local Russian Orthodox Church and pray that my Kostya would be a winner and that he

The loneliness of a new country. Here's Natasha at our first Aussie home at Mascot, showing how she felt when noting: 'I missed my family. I missed Russia. I cried myself to sleep night after night.'

would not be hurt. When it came time for the fight to start, I would leave home and walk quietly along the nearby streets hoping that everything would turn out okay. Sometimes I would return before the fight was over but Timophey would call out, 'Don't come in, Mama, the fight is still on'. And I would turn around and continue my walk.

I don't know what stopped me from turning around and continuing my walk when I arrived home too early during the fight against Ricky Hatton. I had come home and it was, I think, the seventh round. I had this gut feeling that all was not well and I just couldn't leave. I was proved right. It was awful to watch, especially when Kostya was hit with the low blow which doubled him up. That was so hard to take. I could feel his pain from halfway across the world. I thought to myself, 'Oh no, it's happening again'. When Johnny Lewis stopped him from going out for the last round I was so relieved — even more so when I heard Kostya talking after the bout and offering Ricky any help he needed in the future. Kostya looked so battered but it was the real Kostya offering friendship to opponents — warriors he would call them — who had fought bravely. But no one could have fought with greater bravery than Kostya.

When they all arrived home, I was at Sydney Airport and I rushed up and hugged Johnny Lewis, thanking him for saving my Kostya. Johnny knew another round could have endangered him. He could see the warning signs in Kostya's eyes. The eyes were open but they weren't seeing. Johnny is like a second father to Kostya and didn't want to see his 'son' hurt. I will always be in Johnny's debt for that decision he made in Manchester.

PAUL UPHAM

One of Australia's best known boxing photojournalists. He is the editor of the Australian Boxing Almanac *and a contributor to* The Fist *magazine and the American boxing website SecondsOut.com. Paul has also appeared on air for television networks including Main Event, Sky Channel, Fox Sports and SBS.*

SOMETHING VERY SPECIAL

When you have been a winner throughout your professional boxing career, dealing with a loss is a painful experience. For Kostya Tszyu, his defeat at the hands of Ricky Hatton was a strange experience. As an amateur boxer representing the Soviet Union, he was only defeated on 11 occasions while recording 259 wins. His only previous defeat as a professional was at the hands of Vince Phillips five years earlier. And Kostya has always thanked the American for that loss, saying that it made him become a true professional in his preparation and helped him become the undisputed world champion. But after 14 successful world title defences over two separate reigns as a super lightweight world champion — a total of nine years of his life — Kostya had to deal with defeat and deciding on his future, with his career balancing delicately between fighting on and retirement.

It was a brutal battle in Manchester with both men taking incredible punishment. From ringside, it was clear that both fighters gave every ounce of what they had physically, mentally and emotionally in an attempt to win. After it was over, the respect both men showed for each other and their chosen sport was a lesson for not only all boxers, but sportspeople in all pursuits from around the world. As they embraced in the middle of the ring Kostya told Ricky: 'If you ever need any help or advice I'll give you my phone number. I'll be there for you.' Ricky's reply: 'That's not a champion, that's a champion and a half.'

Asking the xenophobic crowd to be quiet, Kostya told them: 'I am a proud man. I am a very, very proud man. I'm not saying this is the end of my career … maybe yes … maybe no … but I am saying that today I lost to the better fighter. There is no shame for me to say this.'

Not everyone can handle defeat so honourably.

On the afternoon after the fight, members of Team Tszyu gathered in their hotel for a private dinner of seafood and copious amounts of the finest Russian vodka. As Tszyu and his father Boris sat side by side, arms around each other, there were speeches of appreciation for the beaten hero. In many ways it was like a wake for the passing of a good friend.

Around 24 hours later, Ricky, his father Ray and members of the Hatton entourage travelled to Kostya's training camp in Wigan to say farewell. While Kostya smiled and posed for pictures, signed souvenir items for Ricky and his team, even giving the newly crowned world champion a copy of his autobiography with its own personal inscription, the now former champion was hurting. While his body was aching from the physical punishment he had sustained, what was hurting most was the realisation he was no longer the undisputed champion of the world.

Before the Hatton fight, a dinner for Kostya had been planned for the Panthers World of Entertainment in Penrith, west of Sydney. Nearly 400 people had bought tickets expecting to pay homage to the returning champion. Kostya could have called off the dinner and no one would have complained, but he elected to attend because he appreciates his fans so much. Battered and bruised, it would not be easy to face his supporters less than a week after suffering a loss that was witnessed by millions of people around the world but Tszyu pressed on. He waited backstage as his theme music 'Something Worth Fighting For' was played. And as he emerged and stood before them, the fans gave him a standing ovation. You could see Kostya lift as the applause carried across the stage. The smile on his face showed how much it meant to him.

When it came time for the audience to ask Kostya questions, so many of them didn't want to. They just stood up and told him how much they loved him and how proud they were of him.

Kostya refused to make any excuses for his loss.

'You cannot win everything in life,' he told the fans. 'It is just impossible. Many people, when they get defeated they lose themselves. But life goes on. Yes, it's not easy. It's very hard. Still, you have to live. You have to continue in life and be proud. That's the reason why I am here tonight and why my kids are still proud of what I did.'

That night at Panthers was something very special. Natasha would later explain: 'This was good for Kostya … to help him.'

Kostya then went away to ponder his future.

But regardless of what his decision would be, the loss to Ricky Hatton could never take away what Kostya has achieved during a lifetime in the ring. One night does not make a legendary career and one night can never take away something so wonderfully special and unique that is Kostya Tszyu — his reputation as a great champion in every sense of the word.

RAY CHESTERTON

The respected veteran sporting columnist with the Sydney Daily Telegraph *newspaper, Ray Chesterton wrote this piece after my fight with Ricky Hatton. His media colleagues regard it as a classic piece of journalism.*

GALLANTRY AND HONOUR

It happens in sport that defeat sometimes gives more than it takes. It can make idols out of the vanquished and leave winners merely admired. A gesture, a word or a look is all it might take for a beaten athlete to endear themselves forever to the public.

Kostya Tszyu is a prime example. He has injected nobility into a sport that more often has wanton barbarism as its emblem. Beaten senseless by Ricky Hatton in losing his world title, Tszyu was the personification of grace under fire in the immediate aftermath in the ring.

'Kostya came to me and said: "You were the better man. You deserved to win",' Hatton said. 'He then said: "If you ever need any help or advice I'll give you my phone number. I'll be there for you." That's not a champion, that's a champion and a half.'

Graciousness does happen in sport, especially golf. Men who have just watched millions of dollars and prestige slide by because of a poor shot or an exceptional one by an opponent, swallow the pain and congratulate the winner. It happens in rugby league too, as evidenced by the Arthur Summons-Norm Provan embrace that became a statue on the Premiership trophy. And there was the iconic example of Australian sportsmanship in 1956 when champion runner John Landy stopped during a mile race that counted toward Olympic selection, to help fallen colleague Ron Clarke. Landy went on to win.

But it is one thing to be courteous after a non-contact sport when only exhaustion, disappointment and a lost dream are demanding salve. Contact sports are different and nothing defines contact sport like the brutality of boxing.

Kostya had been bashed and pummelled for 11 ferocious rounds. His head was swollen like a bloated melon, his glazed eyes stared at nothingness, his cheek was distorted from what was first thought to be a broken jaw and kidney blows caused blood in his urine. He had worked himself into such a detached state of exhaustion against Hatton he was unable to even respond to questions about his condition.

To behave with the chivalry Kostya displayed in those circumstances transcends manners that can be learnt. Such humanity has to be so deeply etched in the psyche it is as natural as breathing.

In the harsh world of competitive sport Kostya has lost his title. In the world in which most of us live he radiates sportsmanship, gallantry and honour as few before him have done.

'In the world in which most of us live [Kostya] radiates sportsmanship, gallantry and honour as few before him have done'

Ray Chesterton

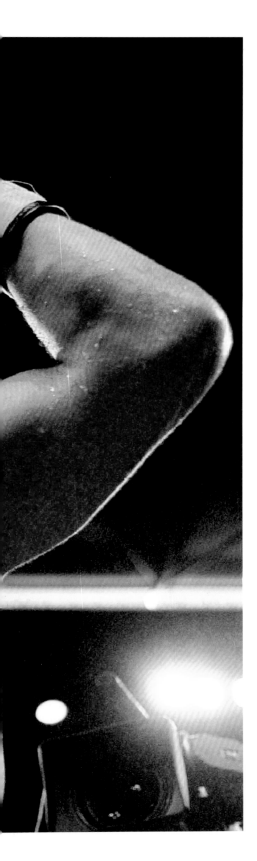

EPILOGUE

BACK HOME AFTER THE HATTON FIGHT, I fulfilled a commitment to appear at a dinner attended by about 400 fans at Panthers World of Entertainment at Penrith, of Sydney.

It had originally been planned as a celebration. And despite my loss, it certainly wasn't a wake. I apologised to my fans but they would hear no words of apology. Their standing ovation almost brought tears to my eyes.

I told them how, no matter who you are, you can't win everything in life — that's just impossible. But life goes on and you have to do something with that life and to keep your pride. That was the reason I was standing at the dinner talking to my fans. And that was the reason why my kids are proud of what I have done.

The day after the dinner I admitted myself to a Sydney hospital for routine tests to ensure there had been no ill-effects from the fight. Imagine my shock when I then read a story by journalist Paul Kent in the Sydney *Daily Telegraph* newspaper under the headline 'Kostya suffers bruising on brain'. Kent had spoken to me and I told him I was fine and had no problems. He used my quotes in the story — but people who saw the headline would have been left with the impression that I was in a bad way.

Dr Bill Anseline, a trusted member of my team, tried to put the record straight: 'I can say categorically there was no bruising in or on Kostya's brain and it would be misleading for anyone to say so. The series of routine scans and tests were purely a precautionary measure.'

The night the story appeared I invited around 30 members of my family and members of Team Tszyu to join me for dinner at a Russian restaurant in the south-eastern Sydney suburb of Kingsford. There was no special reason for the dinner except the fact we were all friends and enjoy each other's company.

I pointed out that because of a sensationalised headline there were millions of people around Australia thinking that there was something wrong with me. My friends and family could see how wrong the media could sometimes be.

Many people have commented on how gracious I was in defeat … how I was a perfect role model for others in acknowledging that I had been beaten by the better fighter on the night. But that is the way I have been taught to live life. Life is not always about winning. You have to carry on after a setback … carry on after a loss. That's the way my Papa taught me and that's the way I have tried to teach my children … encourage them to do the right thing no matter on which stumbling block they falter. Don't put your head down, no matter how low you feel. Be positive. Realise that everything that happens in life happens for a very good reason. What happens is meant to be!

'Life is not always about winning. You have to carry on after a setback'

Kostya

Published by ABC Books for the
AUSTRALIAN BROADCASTING CORPORATION
GPO Box 9994 Sydney NSW 2001

Photographic credits

Cover: Andrew Jacobs/ACP

Back cover: Chris McGrath/Allsport/Getty Images

Inside: AAP: AAP/Dean Lewins 70, 178; AAP/AP/Rick Rycroft 92, 98; AAP/Brendan Esposito 96b;
AAP/AP/Donna Connor 100; AAP/AP/Allen Oliver 103; AAP/AP/Desert Sun/Wade Byars 105; AAP/AFP/Mike
Fiala 110; AAP/AFP/John Gurzinksi 113, 118, 120; AAP/AP/Lori Cain 117, 119; AAP/AP/Steve Holland 121;
AAP/AP File 136, 137; AAP/AFP 172/173

Ern McQuillan: 71, 72t, 72b, 79, 93, 94, 95t, 95b, 96t, 97t

Getty Images: Cameron Spencer/Getty Images 37b; Holly Stein/Allsport/Getty Images 74, 76; Ray Fisher/Time
Life Pictures/Getty Images 81; Getty/Eliot J. Schechter /Allsport 107; John Gurzinksi/AFP/Getty 114;
Keystone/Hulton Archive/Getty Images 136; Mark Nolan/Getty Images 138, 139; Tatyana
Makeyeva/AFP/Getty Images 144tr

Jay Larkin: 112

Newspix: Newspix/Sam Ruttyn 4, 55b; Newspix/Mark Graham 6; Newspix/Glen Cameron 44; Newspix/Milan
Scepanovic 55t, 183; Newspix/Bob Barker 58, 61, 63; Newspix/File 60b, 66; Newspix/Peter Ward 62, 188;
Newspix/NickCubbin 78ml; Newspix/Graham Hely 85; Newspix/Jeff Darmanin 88; Newspix/Michael
Amendolia 102; Newspix/Brett Costello 116, 171; Newspix/Dan Peled 146b; Newspix/Fiona Hamilton 149t;
Newspix/Renee Nowytarger 157; Newspix/John Grainger 176; Newspix/Bob Finalyson 187

Paul Upham: 2, 9, 10, 33, 51, 84, 122, 123tl, 125, 131tr, 142b, 146tl, 147b, 148tl, 148tr, 148b, 150/151, 152t,
152m, 152b, 153b, 154/155, 156tl, 156tr, 156b, 158, 163, 164, 166tr, 166b, 167mr, 167ml, 167br, 168t,
168b, 169t, 169m, 169b, 185, 191, backflap

Sport the Library 73, 89; **Sport the library/ Action Images** 175, 177

Tszyu Private Collection: 12, 14, 15, 16, 17tl, 17tr, 17b, 18, 19, 20, 20/21, 21, 22, 25, 26, 27, 28, 29, 30, 31,
32t, 32b, 34, 36t, 36b, 37t, 37r, 37m, 38, 39, 40, 41t, 42tr, 42bl, 42br, 43t, 43b, 46, 48, 49, 50, 52, 54t,
57, 59, 68, 78tl, 79tr, 78br, 79, 82, 82/83, 83, 86, 90, 97b, 99106, 108, 109, 123ml, 123bl, 123br, 126,
128tl, 128tr, 128br, 129l, 129r, 130tl, 139mr, 130bl, 130br, 131tr, 131b, 132/133, 140, 141t, 141b, 142t,
143t, 143b, 144tl, 144br, 145t, 146ml, 146mr, 147t, 149b, 153t, 161, 166tl, 179, 182, backflap

Key to legend: t=top, tl=top left, tr=top right, m=middle, ml=middle left, mr=middle right, b=bottom,
bl=bottom left, br=bottom right

ISBN 0 7333 1598 4

Design and typesetting by Nanette Backhouse, saso content & design
Set in Glasgow Light 11.5/16
Colour reproduction by PageSet, Victoria
Printed in Hong Kong, China by Quality Printing